HIS GOD, MY GOD

Caroline Urquhart

Bridge Publishing, Inc.
Publishers of:
LOGOS • HAVEN • OPEN SCROLL

Acknowledgments

My grateful thanks are extended to Jane Collis, who has shared the task of writing this book with me, for her love and patience and writing ability. Especially I would like to thank my husband, Colin, our children and the household who have encouraged me; also to Esther, Elaine, Annette and Dick who have ably typed and corrected the manuscript.

His God, My God

Copyright © 1983 by Caroline Urquhart. First printed 1983. All rights reserved. No part of this publication may be reproduced or transmitted in any form or by any means, electronic or mechanical, including photocopy, recording, or any information storage and retrieval system, without permission in writing from the publisher. Printed in Great Britain for Hodder and Stoughton Limited, Mill Road, Dunton Green, Sevenoaks, Kent by Wm. Collins, Glasgow. Photoset by Rowland Phototypesetting Limited, Bury St. Edmunds, Suffolk. Hodder and Stoughton Editorial Office: 47 Bedford Square, London WC1B3DP. American Edition published by Bridge Publishing, Inc., South Plainfield, New Jersey 07080 U.S.A. Printed in the United States of America. Library of Congress Catalog Card Number: 84-70053, International Standard Book Number: 0-88270-566-0. Published by arrangement with Edward England Books.

Contents

1. Is Colin There? 1
2. It's All God's Fault 15
3. No Escape 25
4. Seeking God 35
5. Help! 53
6. In it Together 65
7. Moving on 77
8. Living With God—First Class 93
9. The Hyde 107
10. Revelation at Last 123
11. Hallelujah! 137

Dedication

In praise to my God who has revealed himself to me as my faithful Father and heavenly "Husband."

1

Is Colin There?

Several rooms away, downstairs, the telephone rang yet again. Immediately the whining of the dog rose to meet the volume of the ring and the nerve-grating duet began. It must have been the third time this morning. Why did Blue react like this? His howl was insistent, and certainly wouldn't stop until I picked up the receiver. I scooped up eight-month-old Andrea and ran.

On the landing a toy car race was in full swing, but I managed not to trample on Clive or any of the elaborate track he had set out. Stepping awkwardly over the child barrier at the top of the stairs I ran down them, trying to control Andrea's wrigglings.

"Oh, shut up, Blue!" I snapped at the dog, passing him in the hall. It had no effect, and just made me feel more irritated. At last I reached the study door and almost threw myself at the phone. Blissful silence.

"St. Hugh's Vicarage." My best calm, business-like tone.

"Is the Reverend Urquhart there, please?"

HIS GOD, MY GOD

"No, not at the moment, I'm afraid. Can I take a message for you?" Andrea was now struggling hard, and began to voice her protest at being held. I wedged the receiver under my chin while I placed her on the floor, but too late. The voice of the caller was drowned in her wail. Through it I shouted rather obviously. "Sorry, I can't hear you, just a minute . . ." and abandoned the telephone without knowing whether the message had got through or not.

I grabbed a piece of paper for her to play with: she was easily quieted.

"I'm so sorry about that. Can I help?"

Ah, here was a situation I could control, at last. I reached for a pen and note-pad to take the name of the undertaker, name and address of the next of kin to be visited and all the other information Colin would need. Feeling more efficient in this frequently recurring situation, I replaced the receiver in a calmer mood.

Shriek! Slap! Ow! The cries of incipient battle had me running up the stairs almost faster than I had come down, but it was no more than a routine skirmish and was over before I reached the landing. The luckless Claire, less adept than I at covering the obstacle race of the car track, had caught her foot in the wall of bricks serving as a crash barrier. Clive's roar of indignation seemed quite out of proportion, especially in view of the number of times he would stage a crash deliberately at that point and painstakingly rebuild the wall without a murmur.

"She didn't do it on purpose Clive. Don't be silly."

Is Colin There?

"Well, she'd better not do it again," he grumped. Claire's back paused slightly in its retreat into the bedroom.

"Stupid cars, anyway."

There was no reaction from Clive, so I decided further intervention was unnecessary. Hitching Andrea up more firmly onto my hip, I went into the bedroom and sat down on the edge of our unmade bed. The day had hardly started, and I was exhausted.

We had moved to the parish of St. Hugh's in Luton about six months before. When we had arrived, I had plunged into a fog of constant tiredness and chaos. Andrea was as demanding as any new-born inevitably is, and the house was so much bigger than any we had lived in previously. A sense of inadequacy dogged me all the time; I felt trapped in the house. Often, as with this morning, a sense of hopelessness settled down around me.

Survival. That's what it was all about. Coping until Colin got back for lunch. Cleaning the large downstairs room to be ready for the church meeting tonight even if upstairs it was impossible to put a foot down without standing on something. Long-term plans were bound to end in failure before the day was out, so I just tried to survive a few hours at a time.

In some ways this was a positive attitude, I told myself, but the implied defeat continued to drain what little self-confidence I had. Surely anyone else could cope better in my place. I imagined other mothers to be far more capable. They planned a week at a time and made lists, carrying them out to the letter and leaving time to start knitting Christmas presents in September. These mental images dogged me constantly and made me feel depressed beyond measure.

Quite unconsciously I had been jogging Andrea up and down on my knees, and I suddenly realized she was beaming at me. I grinned back. Perhaps it was all worth it, after all. Clasping her to me in a long bear hug, I set off for the kitchen, which seemed as good a place as any to start.

The smile on the unformed features indicated a good mood, and she gurgled an accompaniment throughout the breakfast washing up, waving a rattle at me from her little chair. Then I got to work on the windowsill behind the sink, which was irritating me. So many tea strainers, milk bottle tops and dish cloths seemed to drift in that direction and I knew it looked so messy from the path.

I had just finished when a prospective admirer of my work appeared round the corner, saw me through the window and headed for the door. He caught my startled movement and smiled. My return smile might have been more enthusiastic. "Oh, no! Not someone else wanting Colin! Would I have to invite him in?" I was still drying my hands when the door bell went, and just found time to kick a few bits of Lego out of view as I went to open the door.

"Is Colin there, please?"

I glanced at my watch. "I'm afraid I'm not expecting

Is Colin There?

him for another hour, at least. Can I help you at all, or take a message?"

"No, no . . . that's very kind." The poor man suddenly looked very unsure of himself, shuffling a foot on the gravel and looking down at it. "It was just something I heard him saying the other day . . . . He wasn't talking to me anyway. I'll think about it a bit more, and then make an appointment to see him. My name is Woodward. It was just that . . . ."

His voice tailed off again. I stood there feeling hopeless; I could offer him nothing. It was Colin, as always, who was needed.

"I'll tell Colin you called, Mr. Woodward." That decided him.

"Thank you very much." He smiled at me, and set off down the path. I closed the door, grateful that he had asked nothing of me. I had to get on. I was fed up with people wanting Colin. He was in constant demand, and never in when they wanted him. I always had to stop what I was doing and try to sort them out.

Although I was a vicar's wife I had no desire to be involved in my husband's work. Naturally, I would take an interest in what he was doing. His parochial responsibilities were his job and I didn't resent that, but what little time was left belonged to the family. When he was home, he was home; the parish was shut outside the door and we could enjoy some family life together.

However, in this fairly new parish something different was happening. People, including Colin, were changing all around me. It soon became painfully obvious that I was the only one who was not changing. I found myself fighting the feelings of resentment at the good things which were happening to others. They were finding a new peace and joy in their lives and I was living with turmoil and depression. I wanted to be a part of it and yet I didn't. I was frightened. What was it all about?

People seemed to enjoy deeper friendships: when they met they embraced one another with obvious affection—rather different from the polite handshake of most church-going people. I couldn't deny that there was a new kind of love between them, but I didn't understand it.

And then there was all the God talk! People seemed to speak about Him freely, something I had never been able to do. What was even more disconcerting was that the way they talked made it clear that God was real to them. They called it "being filled with the Spirit" and "God living in us." They even claimed that He answered their prayers, and many people seemed to have actually been healed from physical illness in miraculous ways.

How could I be a part of all this? Going to church was a duty, and prayer something kept for times of trouble. I didn't want to stop what was going on, but I felt totally excluded, and the worst of it was that Colin, my own husband, was at the center of it all . . . .

Claire came into the kitchen having either cured all the patients in her doll's hospital or left them to their

Is Colin There?

fate. "Mum, can I have a biscuit, please?"

"But it's nearly dinner time, darling. Can't you wait?"

"I don't know. What is it?"

"Shepherd's pie. You like that, don't you?"

"Can we have baked beans?"

"Yes, of course. We'll have it as soon as Daddy gets in. That won't be long now."

"But what can I do while I'm waiting?"

"Why not go and play on the climbing frame? It's nice and warm outside."

"All right. Tell me when Daddy comes." She slipped through the door again and closed it behind her. Now I could get on.

Through the french window I could see Claire squirming around on the climbing frame. Upstairs another hapless racing driver took a nose dive over a high bank at great speed and plunged to unspeakable doom. But no, the fire engine was on its way. Perhaps it was an ambulance siren howling its way to the scene. A great screeching of brakes, a short busy-sounding pause, then the engine roared off, presumably to the hospital. That was one thing you could say for Clive— he never lacked imagination, or volume when it came to sound effects. So two out of the three were occupied, and Andrea was sleeping soundly in her pram.

"I don't seem to have achieved anything yet," I mused as I poked around in the fridge looking for the remains of yesterday's fruit pie. Colin had a clear idea of how things could go wrong, and never made me feel

HIS GOD, MY GOD

as if I should be doing better. It was my own standards I could never live up to, which condemned me at every turn. Deciding my priorities seemed an impossible task. There seemed so much to do. Lunch time was approaching fast, the washing needed to be put into the machine, and I still hadn't made the beds.

At least the potatoes were on the stove before a painstaking but fairly steady clomping down the stairs, followed by a more bumbling run across the hall and a crashing through the door announced the arrival of Clive, whose stomach also reckoned it was dinner time.

"Go outside with Claire for a few minutes, and I'll tell you when Daddy comes," I promised. "He won't be long now." At that moment Andrea woke. I shall need to change her diaper before lunch, was my next thought.

When Colin returned the kitchen was deserted, the only signs of life were the sound of two squabbling children on the climbing frame and indignant screams from upstairs where Andrea was objecting to my ministrations.

Hearing his cheerful "hello" as he came through the door, I tried to hurry up but only seemed to fumble the more. I was grateful that by the time I got downstairs he had hugged Claire back into a peaceful frame of mind, rescued Clive from where he was stuck at the top of the apparatus, and organized them into counting out knives and forks for the table. He greeted me with a kiss. His love was such a relief to me in the middle of

Is Colin There?

all my confusion. I only hoped that he wouldn't start talking about the latest miracles that would have inevitably taken place. I turned away quickly to look for the tin of beans.

"What have you lot been up to this morning?" he asked lightly of the company in general. The chatter from the children at least meant I didn't have to reply. Did he really understand how depressed and threatened I felt? If he did, he certainly couldn't provide any answers, or none I would listen to, anyway.

"Did you manage to pick up the cups and saucers?" I asked. I meant to show informed interest in the evening's meeting for which they were needed, but of course it came out too hard, like an accusation.

"No, I thought I would have more time this afternoon, and anyway, I knew the kids would be wanting their lunch."

"While I remember, there are several messages on your desk, and a Mr. Woodward called, but is going to phone again for an appointment." Now I was sounding like a secretary, not a wife.

"O.K. Fine. Sounds as though you've been busy."

"No worse than usual. What sort of morning have you had?" Oh, blow! That fatal question slipped out.

"Great. The Lord has been busy as usual. Three people from the last group were filled with the Spirit and we had a couple of really significant healings too."

"Oh, yes," I said, knowing how flat and unenthusiastic my answer must have sounded. But Colin was now well away, pouring out the details of the latest mighty works. I knew that he had to share his excitement with someone and that person should be me. Try as I might, I could never respond with even a flicker of emotion.

And yet I was confronted with the reality that God heals, even within my own family. Andrea had been born with incompletely formed hip joints. The doctors said at first that she would have to spend several months in a frame and when a little older would need a series of operations. I knew Colin was praying for her and I couldn't account for the fact that two weeks later it was found that nothing was wrong with her hip joints at all. But I regarded that as an answer to Colin's faith. It certainly couldn't have been an answer to mine!

"The Lord deals uniquely with each person," Colin was saying. "That's what I find so great and so challenging. You have to listen carefully to what He is saying in each situation. God moves in one way when you are praying with one person, and then in a completely different way with another. Still, He knows everything about us, the ways in which we need to be changed and healed."

I stayed silent. I didn't want God to change my life. Oh, I would have been quite happy for things that I didn't like about myself to be changed, and goodness knows there were plenty of them, but I would do it myself. That way I could stay in control. My lack of response to Colin's conversation checked his enthusiasm.

"I can tell you another time if you're waiting to serve up." The excitement had gone out of his voice, and I

Is Colin There?

could see him thinking, "Oh, help. I've said too much again."

"No, no. Do finish. If you could just sort out the drinks for the children . . . ."

"Oh, it doesn't matter," he said lamely. "Where have those kids gone at the last minute?" It was an evasion, but Colin seemed to be as grateful as I was to change the subject. He noticed they were back on the climbing frame, and went to tap on the window.

I was looking to see that everything was on the table when I suddenly felt him behind me, reaching a tentative arm round my waist. I had hurt him, and he wanted to check that I was all right. For a moment I leant back against him, feeling his strength and love, but I wasn't ready to answer questions. He nuzzled against my ear, and I put my hands over his, wanting to reassure him. Then the children burst in, and I unwrapped myself with more speed than necessary, hurting him again. I just couldn't cope with his affection when I felt like this. I didn't understand him any more. His news seemed to be a barrier between us, not a bridge, and I was sure it was my fault.

Coping with the children and listening to their chatter allowed my mind, or at least my feelings, to go back into the dark hole they had crept out of. The shepherd's pie hadn't really warmed through properly, and the beans had stuck to the saucepan and dried out. I might as well have been eating straw. I couldn't face the fruit pie as well, and was pleased that Andrea still had to be fed. By the time she was settled in her pram, Colin had done the washing up and made coffee. Surely he had to be somewhere else, didn't he? His parishioners always seemed to have first claim on his attention. Things happened to them, and they changed. I was forever the same, forever in a muddle, never getting anywhere. He, however, had obviously decided to sit down for a quiet chat together.

"I suppose we'll have to do the grass again at least once more. It still seems to be growing quite fast." Not a bad attempt, I thought. One better than the weather.

"Yes, I'll have a go some time tomorrow, if it's not raining."

Silence.

"How many are you expecting for tonight? I'll try to get the chairs out."

"Oh, about twenty-five, I suppose, but don't bother. The children will need the room to run around when it gets too cold to be outside later."

"Well, I'll see how the afternoon goes."

"Have they been getting on top of you today? You seem a bit low."

"Oh, I don't know." I sighed heavily. "I haven't had time to work it out, but I do feel fed up again. I thought I was getting better at last."

"Don't worry about it. It will pass. You'll only make yourself feel guilty about it, and that wouldn't help." I glanced up and tried to return his smile. From inside, it felt like more of a grimace and I knew it didn't fool Colin.

"That's better. Why don't you enjoy what might be

Is Colin There?

the last week of sunshine? Take the children to the park and they can let off steam kicking dead leaves about. Perhaps you could go and see someone."

"That's an idea. I might just do that, but I'll have to do some washing first."

"Make sure you get out for a while. Promise?"

He smiled again, and I suddenly felt tears pricking my eyes. How lovely it would be if all I needed was fresh air! I swept the empty cups up off the coffee table between us and made for the door.

"O.K. I promise."

As I fussed around in the kitchen doing nothing, I was aware that Colin was sitting quietly. Goodness knows what he was thinking. At last he got up heavily and went to the study to collect something for the afternoon. A few moments later he called out. "See you darling. Have a good time." The door closed and I was alone again.

As soon as he had passed the kitchen window, I leaned against the table and closed my eyes, squeezing them tight to hold back the tears.

"Have a good time," he said.

2

It's All God's Fault

By the time we reached the park the sunlight was rather pale and watery, and something stronger than a breeze meant we had to keep moving to stay warm. Of course, the older two were rushing around like mad things anyway, Clive pedalling away on his trike and Claire darting ahead with Blue and then coming back to "have a go" with the pram. For a while I tried to keep both of them and the dog in my vision the whole time, but as we moved away from the road I stopped worrying so much. Clive was quite capable of abandoning his trike in the middle of the path if something else attracted his attention, so I sometimes found myself maneuvering both pram and trike together, but apart from that, I let myself enjoy the walk.

Perhaps Colin was right. I had always found it easier to stay in the house than make the effort to go out and make friends. It was always such a struggle to get the children ready to go out. Still, there was no doubt that they loved this spell of freedom in the park, and so did Blue.

HIS GOD, MY GOD

As I walked, my thoughts continued to whirl. If God has chosen Colin for such a ministry, why has He allowed me to marry him? I'm a spiritual failure. I'm not sure I believe in God, let alone know Him or expect Him to answer prayers. But I have to pull myself together. I mustn't be a burden to Colin. He must not come home fearing what situation he's going to meet. Are his protestations that I'm not a failure what he truly thinks, or is he trying to humor me along?

We had always been honest with each other and neither of us spoke false or flattering words to the other. But there were times when I so needed encouragement. Because I had such a low opinion of myself I found it difficult to believe the loving things Colin said to me. Perhaps he really understood my need and was saying what I needed to hear. Certainly he had grown even more affectionate recently, and wanted to share in some way the cloud which was hovering over me. When I refused to talk about it with him, he accepted that and was still ready to help in any way he could.

Six years of marriage had brought a great sense of teamwork, and sometimes getting through the practicalities of life absorbed me so much I forgot, or took for granted, the depth of affection which lay behind this. Most couples were like that, I supposed.

What about all these stories of miracles then? If I took out the element of "what God had done" they seemed less threatening. But how could I do that? Colin obviously thought "what God had done" was central to all these events.

It's All God's Fault

I had been confirmed as a girl, but was woefully ignorant about the Bible and who God was supposed to be. Colin's talk about Him affecting everyday situations seemed totally unrelated to my understanding of God. I couldn't accept the familiarity of relationship with Him that Colin often implied. He tried to be sensitive when talking to me, but I knew from the way he spoke in sermons that he believed everyone should have a personal relationship with God. He kept saying that Jesus had made that possible. But how? That was what I could not grasp.

Colin himself had changed so much. About the time Andrea was born, he was constantly excited about something or other. From that time on there had been a new note of authority in his preaching and a new confidence in his work as well as all this love that I found so difficult to relate to. Somehow with a new baby and a new house to cope with I was wrapped up in my own world and felt excluded from what had happened to him. The question was whether I wanted to be part of it. I couldn't understand it at all; it was beyond me, and, in a sense, frightened me.

I shivered. The wind was colder now, and I didn't feel like visiting anybody. I would go home. It was easier.

Blue was quite easy to catch and clip back on to the lead: he had run himself down. Claire volunteered to take the pram again and I was free to marshal them along the pavement of the quite busy road. It was just as well it wasn't far. Clive was pedalling more and more slowly, and I was looking forward to a cup of tea.

HIS GOD, MY GOD

As we neared the house, I realized someone was on the doorstep, presumably ringing the bell. They turned away, and I almost wondered whether to walk more slowly and hope they would go without seeing us, when I saw it was Betty.

"Betty! Just a minute. How lovely to see you." How did this wonderful woman know when to turn up? She was one of the few people I could have faced at that moment. Like a sort of fairy godmother she could cope with any number of children at once, comforting and scolding where necessary, and almost mothering me, her presence was so reassuring.

"Hello, Caroline. I thought I'd missed you. Here, let me take Blue while you find your keys. And how's my Claire? Looking after Andrea for Mummy? You've done a good job—she's fast alseep. Clive, you'd better not take your trike in like that, the wheels are all muddy. And your shoes. Let's take them off." With a few waves of her wand we were in, coats off, kettle on, drinks for children and dogs provided, and my little cloud of despondency gently rebuked and slipping away.

"You're still looking tired, Caroline. You drive yourself too hard. You ought to let up a bit and do something you enjoy."

"Oh, there isn't really anything I want to do. My idea of heaven is a day where I have some peace and quiet so I can catch up with the housework."

"Well, it's not good enough. You're more than just a mother and a housewife, you're a person."

It's All God's Fault

"But, Betty, there's no time."

"Thank goodness we don't all have to live up to your standards. Your children are always clean and neat, the house is always clean under the toys, and you have to cope with half the parish on your doorstep as well." She caught my dismissive shrug. "No, I mean it. You're doing a good job, and don't let anyone tell you any different."

"How can you say that? You're much better at it than I am."

"Of course I am. I breeze in here, full of the energy you've used up getting through the morning. Anybody can do it for an hour at a time. I'm not up several times in the night, nor am I feeding a baby. No wonder it gets on top of you. You ask too much of yourself. No, don't worry about putting the cookies on a plate. I know what a cookie tin looks like."

I took a sip of tea and leaned back into the sofa. The combined effort of Betty and the tea was a real tonic.

"Betty, you're so reassuring. I was in a right stew. I feel better now."

"Good. How's that busy husband of yours?"

"Busy."

"Bound to be. He's really got the parish on the move now, but it means a lot of extra work for him. There's another 'Know Jesus' group tonight, isn't there?"

"Yes, it must be getting towards the end of the series. I think they finish next week."

"Already! I've really been enjoying it, and I've learned so much. Have you been able to go at all yet?"

HIS GOD, MY GOD

"No, not yet." I realized my answer sounded blunt. "I'll go one of these days, I suppose. At the moment it just seems like another thing to cope with."

"Yes, I'm sure. How about if I looked after the children so that you could go to a course? Things are already changing in my life simply through hearing the teaching. I'm beginning to feel like a new woman."

"You certainly all seem to be full of it at the end of the evening." I was on the defensive again, and a sardonic note had crept into my voice. Betty smiled.

"It must be difficult to understand from the outside. You really should come and try some time."

"But won't people think it a bit odd? I mean, won't they think I should know already?"

"Oh, yes," Betty smiled. "Everyone knows Colin spends his day off preaching at his wife!"

"Joking apart, though. What worries me is that I'm not the slightest bit interested."

"Don't feel guilty about it. Lots of people couldn't care less."

"But I'm Colin's wife!"

"Don't push yourself. Everybody at their own time and their own speed, I say. My Bill would have told me where to get off if I'd nagged him into coming."

"Oh, Colin doesn't nag." I thought for a moment. "It's just that he's changed so much himself, I feel I ought to understand why. And all you others."

"What do you mean by that?"

"Well, all this hugging that goes on in church for a start."

It's All God's Fault

"I suppose that as we've come into a new relationship with God, He's given new relationships with each other."

"Sorry, Betty. You're sounding like a sermon. The more of that I hear, the less I want to know about it."

"What you need to hear is what Colin is teaching, straight from the horse's mouth. I'm sure it'll make sense then. If it makes sense to me, it would make sense to anyone."

I couldn't be bothered to argue any more. I knew it wasn't really a question of understanding. I just didn't want to listen. I couldn't face the challenge of this "God business." The conversation moved on, and I relaxed again into the homely details of Betty's life and mine.

All too soon, the children crashed into the room. The cartoon on the television had finished and they were ready for tea.

"I'll be off then, and see you tonight," said Betty, rising to her feet. She gathered the cups together and took them into the kitchen, despite my protests.

"You've got plenty to do without that," she said as she weaved round me.

"Oh, I'll manage." I couldn't admit to anyone how unenthusiastic I was at the thought of producing another meal. "Tea's more or less under control, and Colin will be back soon. We haven't much to get ready before the meeting."

By the time she left, however, I felt as though I could never be ready in time. The end of the day was always difficult. I was tired, the children were irritable and

HIS GOD, MY GOD

wouldn't cooperate, and the mess upstairs made my heart sink. Colin had been delayed somewhere along the line and had to go back out straight after tea to collect the cups and saucers from the church hall. It didn't take long, because it was right next door to the vicarage, but somehow it seemed the last straw. I tackled the bathing with diminished energy, and was unreasonably hard on Claire, who wanted to play for "just five more minutes." When the doorbell announced the first arrival I had to go down and play the smiling hostess; Colin would be absorbed in his preparation for the meeting.

Once everyone was there, I was happy to retreat into the kitchen and attack the huge pile of ironing which had taken up permanent residence in the cupboard. I wouldn't have to face them all again until the coffee break half-way through the meeting. Then again I would have to be the charming, smiling wife! If only they knew how I stood outside the door petrified, plucking up the courage to go in!

Tonight Betty was there, smiling gently at me across the room. How many people there wondered why I never stayed to listen? They probably assumed I had heard it all before. I felt so self-conscious I was always glad to escape from the room. Once out, I stood looking at the ironing for a few minutes, and decided I would put it away. I didn't have the energy.

I was upstairs when the meeting broke up. When I went down to clear up, Colin was still talking to two or three people. The voices went on and on, so when I had dried up and put everything away, I decided to go to bed. I felt left out. I knew it was my decision to be left out, but I wanted Colin to myself, at least for a few minutes, and he was still talking to them. I had no idea who they were, but it didn't matter, they just symbolized the faceless "them" to whom Colin was prepared to devote so much time.

Once in bed, I picked up a book, but I couldn't get back into it, and my eyes were getting heavy. Tomorrow would start soon enough, and there was no reason to suppose it would be any better than today. It certainly wouldn't be if I didn't get some sleep.

"It's all God's fault," I muttered into my pillow. "He's taking my husband away from me."

When Colin came in, despite my desire to "have him to myself," I was three quarters asleep, and not in any state to discuss the weighty issues of the day. I did mumble something to communicate the fact that I wasn't quite asleep, and that earned me a soft kiss. Then the edges of the world blurred, and I drifted off.

3

No Escape

For an astonishing period of eighteen months I continued to ignore the aspects of Colin's ministry I found unacceptable.

Although Colin's life and work had changed, it seemed, in a permanent way, I gradually came to accept the effect it had on our family life, with only the occasional rebellion. Emotionally I still rejected what he was doing, and wanted to know nothing about it, but I couldn't remain totally ignorant forever, however cautious he was about putting his foot in it. As far as I was concerned, our relationship carried on nearly as before. I just cut out of my mind this area of conflict. If he was constantly frustrated in his desire to share more with me, he outwardly continued to support and love me even though I spurned what was so important to him.

One issue, however, could not be ignored, and upset me terribly. It was his hands.

Among the areas Colin was learning about, physical healing was one of the most controversial. People would come to hear his teaching on this subject, and to be healed themselves. Naturally Colin had enthused about this development when it first happened, hoping that such clear signs of God at work would encourage me, but now he kept it more or less to himself. In words, at least.

What he couldn't hide was the unmistakable radiance of his face when he had been ministering to people. Norma, a member of the parish, came to him when the doctors forecast that within six months she would be in a wheelchair for the rest of her life. Her whole body was stiff and movement painful: rheumatoid arthritis, two slipped discs and virus infection in her spinal fluid had been diagnosed. Would Colin help her?

Both she and Colin learned a great deal about healing and about faith over the next few months as they prayed together, often several times a week. It was particularly after he had appointments with her that Colin returned with his face glowing, as if he had been in a hot sun all morning. As he passed the kitchen window he would smile in, looking like an advertisement from a holiday brochure, and I would turn away with dread. When he came in to greet me, the warmth of his hands was unmistakable. Although Colin himself only had enthusiastic words for the way her healing was progressing, that warmth was supernatural, and I couldn't cope with it. However unformed my concept of a powerful and holy God might be, it seemed wrong that the hands through which God had worked should

No Escape

come home and touch me. On several occasions, Norma's joints which had been locked for years would suddenly be freed and move again, first stiffly and then without pain. Colin actually felt bones moving into place as he prayed. Then when he told me, my only response would be, "Oh, yes?"

The God I knew was in heaven, and I didn't expect Him to do very much. Throughout childhood I had turned to Him in desperation when things when wrong, and didn't apparently get answers, and that was about the extent of my faith now. I wasn't used to a God who answered prayers.

Since I couldn't accept Colin's teaching in any other form, it was mainly through his sermons that I understood what was going on. One morning in particular everyone else seemed to gain so much from the sermon, and to me it meant so little. For once I really wanted to get to the bottom of it, but concentration was so difficult with the children to control. In fact, I wondered whether it was worth my going at all. It was often out of a sense of duty and loyalty to Colin that I endured the nightmare of trying to make the three children respectable, prepare the lunch, get ready myself—and all by 9:30 A.M.—only to feel that the whole thing was a waste of time. Other mothers had their husbands to help; but Colin was usually out taking the earlier service and during the service I attended he was naturally always "out front" and never sitting with me to help control the children.

HIS GOD, MY GOD

This morning was a prime example. The children were testing my patience to the limit. Claire seemed to be listening intently, but her eyes were fixed on a spot some way away, under the pew in front. One of Clive's coloring pencils had fallen to the floor and rolled out of reach. I was too late to stop him. His tail end was silently disappearing as Claire and I looked, making his escape towards the end of the pew.

Experience of this sort of procedure had convinced me that the only pew to occupy was the back row. I was less conspicuous and embarrassed there, especially as we usually slipped in at the last minute.

A hasty grab would have provoked a roar of indignation, but I had to intervene quickly. I tapped the only portion of his person I could reach, just to let him know I was aware of what was going on, and he turned round guiltily, too fast, and banged his nose on the heavy wooden pew. So much for my aim to maintain silence. As the crying started I hauled him back on to my lap and tried to console him. It hadn't been much of a bump, but the circumstances of an accident determined Clive's reaction rather than the actual pain inflicted, and in this case frustration was the major emotion. I was probably over-sensitive about the children distracting others. It was true that the congregation were accustomed to children, and didn't seem to take much notice. But at the same time, it was such an effort to try to keep them quiet and amused. Prayer was impossible for me.

The church building, constructed to provide the

No Escape

needs of the housing estate, was very modern, clean and white. Not that I missed plaque-lined walls, pillars and thick, dusty heating pipes. Its simplicity appealed to me and it had a beautiful atmosphere about it. The underfloor heating was effective, and the raised platform for the altar was lit by the high modern stained glass windows which provided a splash of bright color in contrast to the white of the rest of the decor. I had often found a measure of peace as I sat in this building, surrounded by the worshiping congregation, but today I felt only frustration. The little that the children had allowed me to hear didn't make sense, and I didn't enjoy listening to my husband without being able to understand him. At last Colin finished, introduced the next hymn, and the predictability of the Communion Service got under way. But still I could not relax. The tension between the familiar figure of Colin, whom I loved, and the challenging words of the sermon, which I did not want to face, was now replaced with a new tension. How could I say all those words honestly when I wasn't sure whether I believed them? When I looked at them, read them at my own speed rather than speaking out loud with everyone else, I found them challenging and uncomfortable. Having to receive communion only seemed to make things worse. There really wasn't any option about taking communion myself: I was too aware of what others would think if I didn't. The children looked forward to having hands laid on them in blessing. Colin would think something was very wrong, and how many

HIS GOD, MY GOD

others would notice? No need to cause an uproar because I was in a funny mood. I would have to keep up the great pretense.

"Parish Breakfast" was the rather high-flown name given to the cup of tea and cookie we had in the hall attached to the church. For Colin this was always a busy time, and his diary was essential. Names of people who were ill, times and places of meetings, details of new members or visitors were all noted, and there were always many who wanted more than a few minutes with the vicar! My function was usually to be polite to everyone and keep the children under control. I have never been any good at small talk and therefore found it difficult.

This morning, Betty offered to play with all three children and I was once again pleased to lean on her support. Then I realize I would have to find someone to talk to. Seeking safety in numbers, I moved towards a largish group involved in an animated discussion, and listened for a few minutes.

"I just got more and more confused about the whole thing," a very tall young man was saying. "I really wanted to know if I was missing out on what God wanted to give me. It was difficult to discuss with other people, but I thought about it, and suddenly realized that I ought to be asking God. If He wanted to give me something, then I was asking for it and would get it, and if I didn't, then maybe I had misunderstood, although I didn't think so. I read the Bible more and more, and prayed, and realized that I didn't really know what it

No Escape

meant to be a Christian. Above all, this talk of the Holy Spirit had unsettled me. I had been confirmed, hadn't I?

"Anyway, one night after a 'Know Jesus' group, I went home quickly and prayed harder than ever before. It seemed easier than usual. It was more chatting to God than praying. I felt really drawn to Him, and instead of asking for something, I found myself thanking Him for His love. As I did, it was as if a great wave of love swept over me, and words didn't seem adequate any more. I fell into silence, but I wanted more and more to tell God how much I loved Him, and suddenly words came which weren't words. Somehow I knew I was speaking to God in a language He understood, and that this must be 'tongues' although at that point I hadn't really been taught about that, just heard about it vaguely. I use them every day now. That's what it was like for me."

"I don't really see how it helps," began one of his audience, and because I didn't want to become involved, I slipped away. I weaved between lively conversations, some that I couldn't join because they looked too intense and personal, others I couldn't face because of the joyful faces which jarred with my mood. Finally I gave up and went to find Betty again.

"Oh course, you'll be wanting to cook the lunch," she said. "Do tell Colin I really enjoyed his sermon. No, that's a silly thing to say. What I mean is, I got a lot out of it, and I'm going home to write down what I can remember to think about later."

HIS GOD, MY GOD

Not Betty as well, I thought. Suddenly I just had to get out, and so hurriedly thanked her and herded the children towards the door. I felt as though I were in enemy territory, likely to be attacked at any time, and reaching the fresh air was like crossing the border into my own land.

Once inside the house, I turned on the oven and spent a bit of time with the children. Clive, who had spent the better part of two hours awake in the night, was now rather short-tempered, but a few minutes of friendship in building a garage restored relationships. Claire wanted some help in reading a story about a balloon: she knew the plot backwards through having had it read to her again and again, but she was working out some of the longer words and wanted to show me how well she was doing.

I was back in the kitchen by the time I caught sight of movement on the path and realized Colin was on his way. Instinctively I turned my back to the window. Why on earth had I done that? He reached the door and greeted the children noisily in the hall. Knowing he would come in soon, I stood at the sink with my back resolutely turned towards him and waited. He took longer than I expected, and my thoughts ricocheted back and forth.

I hated the way I was reacting. Colin was my mainstay after all. Without him I was lost. How could I open fire on him?

When he came, he came quietly, shutting the kids behind the door. This was a confrontation that

No Escape

couldn't be blurred with other issues. Goodness knows how he had realized something was in the air. How well he knew me!

"My love?" For a moment I held my ground while he stood and waited. Then, with a stifled sob, my hands still wet, I flew across the kitchen and buried my head in his shoulder. We held each other for a long time. I didn't cry, just clung. The only explanation he got that morning was a sigh.

"Oh, Colin!"

4
Seeking God

Perhaps my dependence on Colin was due in part to my home background. I have few memories of my mother. When I was three she went into the hospital leaving the three of us, myself the youngest, in my father's care, and I never saw her again. My childhood was far from unhappy, but my father's remarriage when I was eleven brought a new sense of insecurity and resentment at having to share him. Gradually I overcame this and a good relationship developed with my new mother, Audrey. This was just as well, because it was the only cushion I had against the shock of my father dying when I was twenty.

By that time I was involved in the usual series of boyfriends. Like most girls there were times when there wasn't anybody special, at other times a relationship seemed promising, but only brought disappointment in the end. I worked in a fashion shop in Cambridge, eventually became manager with another company and bought a little car. Now I was independent and mobile; the world was mine to discover. Who could I

HIS GOD, MY GOD

go and see within driving distance for an evening?

Shirley, my cousin's wife, answered the phone.

"That's a lovely idea. Come for supper. Tell you what, if you come on Thursday you can meet our new friend."

"Male or female?"

"What do you think? It's our curate. He often drops in: we get on well with him. I think he might come up to your high standards!"

"Well, we'll see about that. Look, I must go, my lunch hour is over. Shall I come about seven?"

"Oh, whenever you can get here. It'll be lovely to see you."

"Yes, I'm looking forward to it. See you. 'Bye."

The assistant in the shop hooted with laughter at my news.

"A blind date with a vicar! You don't half land yourself in it! What's his name?"

"I don't know a single thing about him, except that John and Shirley like him. Should be good for a laugh at least. 'One lump or two, Vicar?' Anyway, they're not all skinny, short-sighted and moth-eaten, you know."

"I want a full report on Friday morning. Right?"

"You shall have it."

Half-way through the evening, I remembered my promise, and thought about what I could say. Colin was skinny all right, and had come straight from work in his clergy gear with a gray floppy jumper over the top, so he fitted the image. What I hadn't expected, stupidly now I realize, was that he was human, with a

Seeking God

great sense of humor. We had a relaxed, hilarious evening, and I couldn't think of a single joke to crack to Wendy the next day. I skated round it by saying that there wasn't so much as a cucumber sandwich in sight, and then more or less forgot both the jokes and Colin.

A couple of months later, I went to live with Shirley and John for a short while, driving to work from there. The weekend I arrived they were going to a party held by Colin and another curate, who had birthdays close together, so I was invited as well.

As the party progressed, Colin and I spent more and more time with each other, until it was obvious to me that something special was going on. Although I was cautious in conversation with Shirley, inside I was singing loudly. I felt wonderful, Colin was wonderful, life was wonderful.

For the first formal date he took me to the show *Beyond the Fringe* and then for a meal. From that moment there was no doubt in either of our minds that this relationship was very important to both of us. Later, Colin ruefully admitted that the little outing had cost him all of one month's salary! Four or five more modest dates later, we agreed to marry. Our engagement was formally announced a couple of weeks later in April, and the wedding fixed for October.

One incident from the wedding which I remember from time to time was a remark by my godmother to Audrey. Looking across at the radiant couple she asked, prophetically, "Does Caroline know what she's taking on, marrying a vicar?"

HIS GOD, MY GOD

Evidently I didn't. For seven years I had thought our marriage was a good one, and being a vicar's wife wasn't too bad and didn't hold much challenge. But this "baptism in the Spirit" was a great threat to me. All around me people's lives were being changed. At first it seemed to be the super-spiritual ones, later I could see no single common factor. In January 1972, two cases touched me in particular and gave me grounds for much thought.

The first case was that of David and Jane, who were not even members of our church. Originally they had only intended to book the church hall for their wedding reception, but on seeing our nice modern church decided it would be more convenient to have the service there as well. One of them lived in the parish, so they fulfilled that requirement, but Colin had another. For some time now he had stipulated that couples he married should either have attended marriage preparation courses or a "Know Jesus" series. One of the latter was beginning at a convenient time, so they agreed to come. At the end of the teaching time, Colin always made appointments to see each member of the group individually or, in David's and Jane's case, as a couple. During this talk, they discussed the teaching and were asked whether they wanted to know Jesus for themselves. Since they said they did, they were sent off to write down all the things in their life of which they wanted to repent, and all the facets of themselves they were giving to Jesus, both positive and negative. This they did, and on their final

Seeking God

visit, ten days before the wedding, they both together asked Jesus to come into their lives and fill them with His Holy Spirit. Evidently He did. You could see the joy shining from them at this heavenly wedding present. Even I, with all my doubts, was overwhelmed by it.

The second incident puzzled me even more. David and Jane had not been churchgoers, but at least they were capable of a rational decision. When Colin came down from putting the children to bed one night there was great joy tempered with caution in his eyes. He told me that Claire had asked Jesus into her life and had prayed in tongues. She was only six years old.

It must really be very simple, I decided. What was I making such a fuss about? My defenses by this time were very low, and my antagonism wearing thin. After a long discussion one night, Colin asked me if I would like him to pray with me to be filled with the Spirit. I decided I would. I knew enough about it, and was intrigued. It might solve all my problems and bring me closer to Colin.

We knelt together on the carpet. I felt clumsy and awkward, but being on my knees helped to arrange my thoughts into a suitable mood. My heart was beating fast and my face felt flushed. Was this it?

Colin prayed a very simple prayer in English. I said "Amen" and fully intended to pray myself, but was choked and couldn't. After a pause, Colin placed his hands on my head and prayed in tongues aloud for several minutes. The floor was hard under my knees and sitting on my shoes wasn't comfortable after a

HIS GOD, MY GOD

while. I wriggled a bit. Colin paused and caught my eye. My high hopes, which had been faltering, were now completely dashed. Determined, Colin prayed again.

"Father, we thank You for hearing our prayers and leading us up to this point. Continue to guide us both together in Your way. Amen."

I couldn't say "Amen" this time. As far as I was concerned nothing had happened. All I wanted was to be in bed, asleep and unable to think or feel any more. Colin wanted to talk, but I would have nothing to do with him.

I had got the sign I asked for. Now I knew. God had rejected me.

After that evening, the whole subject was taboo again. For several months I pushed it to the back of my mind. Yet slowly I had to recognize that as well as feeling surrounded, as if in enemy territory, I also had mutiny within myself. A small voice inside me was still wanting to find release from my self-made world. At first it was a whisper so low I could only hear it in the stillness of the night when I had been up to comfort Clive. Usually I would be asleep again before I could work out what it was saying. Then events and conversations during the day would prompt me again and again to ask myself whether I could afford to ignore this God.

Eventually I came to the point where I really wanted to tackle the issue. Yet where could I begin? I couldn't concentrate in church, didn't want to go to a "Know

Seeking God

Jesus" group. Somehow I had to get outside of this parish and talk to someone who knew the situation well, and yet wouldn't necessarily expect me to know anything.

"What about Alan?" Colin's question was very hesitant, not wanting to intrude more than was helpful. Alan Woodland had been a curate with Colin in Cheshunt, but the relationship was deeper than a simple partnership in church work. Many hours had been spent together planning, discussing and praying, and although I hadn't been in on all this, I still felt Alan was someone I could trust. He was now in charge of a church nearby, but we had been so engulfed by our new parish, as he by his, that our friendship had rather fallen into abeyance.

The idea grew on me, so I told Colin I would be pleased if he would mention it when he was next in touch. Before I knew where I was, Colin had arranged everything, even changing his day off so he could look after the children while I went over there. I don't know what he had told Alan, but he was obviously thrilled himself.

Our first meeting was to be an exploratory conversation, so that Alan knew what sort of areas we would need to cover. I was pleased to have this opportunity to step outside the situation, but suddenly nervous as I rang the doorbell. Was I about to show myself as a fool?

If Alan had been briefed in advance about the extent of the problem, he showed no signs of complicity as he

HIS GOD, MY GOD

guided me into his study and I was immediately at my ease. Quiet-spoken himself, he was a very good listener and his eyes took in my agitation before I expressed it. From time to time he smiled or nodded, stroking his beard thoughtfully, and I could sense his sympathy.

With this encouragement, I talked for a long time. I wasn't prepared to go into any problems between Colin and myself: loyalty demanded silence on that score. The essence of the question was, "What exactly is going on all around me?" I was very confused in my mind, and all that I said was so overlaid with my emotional reaction it was a wonder he made any sense of it all.

Finally I ground to a halt.

"You've been having a rough time, haven't you, Caroline?"

I grimaced. Then Alan asked straight out, "Tell me, do you believe in God?"

My words tumbled over themselves. "You try living in that vicarage with people being healed of neuroses, cancer and the common cold, and crowds arriving for stupid interminable meetings, grinning like clowns and hugging each other like long-lost cousins. I can't see God, but I'm the only one, so I must be wrong. I've always believed in some sort of being in the sky, but there's obviously more to it than that."

"And do you want to know more?"

"Yes, I think I do now. For a long while I just couldn't

Seeking God

care less, but now it matters to me. More and more. That's why I'm here, I suppose."

"Good. I certainly wouldn't be able to help you unless you were really looking for yourself. I could talk until the cows came home, but if you didn't want to hear, I'd be wasting my time. God never barges in where He isn't wanted."

We agreed to meet on alternate Tuesdays. There was no time limit set, but I somehow always felt that Alan would not have gone forever: once I had grasped enough to make a decision he would talk through that decision and then leave it to me. The ground we were covering was effectively a sort of confirmation class, the basics of what it meant to be a Christian. Between meetings he gave me some "homework" to do: short Bible passages to read, and sometimes a chapter of a book to think about. I found his methodical approach very refreshing and reassuring. For so long I had been hiding doubts and questions, even from myself, because I thought they were unworthy of the loyal wife I wanted to be. Now at last I could pull them out into the open air and give them a good look over. Although they made me more conscious of the spiritual gap betwen Colin and myself, I felt strangely closer to him.

I came back from the third meeting with Alan thrilled at the way everything was fitting together.

"You know that vague God I had up in the sky? Well, I see now that He has done everything possible not to be vague any more. That's why Jesus had to come." A slow smile was growing on Colin's face as he turned to look at me. "And because of Jesus, we can see that God really does love us," I continued triumphantly. "Good, isn't it?"

"I don't believe it." Colin shook his head.

"Well, if you don't believe that, you ought not to wear your collar backwards," I grinned.

"You know perfectly well what I mean," he retorted. "You must have heard what you've just said about sixty times from my mouth, and you come home crowing about it like it was the morning headlines."

"I'm sorry. I was tuned into a different frequency before."

"O.K. I can tell I'm not much good as your vicar. I'll just shut up and concentrate on being your husband." He pulled me towards him.

"Good. I prefer you like that, anyway." We stood holding each other for a long moment. It was like a sigh of relief in our relationship.

Ten days later, on the Friday evening, I decided I would join the group who met for worship in our lounge. Commitment to one another was the subject which seemed to come up again and again. In the morning services, particularly in the sermon, this theme was developed as we explored together. I had been discussing with Alan the new relationships which God wants to have with us, so I suddenly found that loving other Christians seemed to be a logical step. More than that, I suddenly felt quite close to that group of people, felt I was one of them at last.

Then there was a time of open prayer, and the

Seeking God

dreaded clicking of people praying in tongues began. As I listened, my mood switched completely, and the conviction grew that I wasn't one of them. I had sat on the back row so I could slip out without disturbing anyone if the children needed me, and now I took advantage of this. It wasn't any good pretending, I just didn't fit.

When Colin came up to bed, I was reading the Bible passages Alan had set for our next meeting. I could see him putting a very positive construction on the sight, and didn't want him to get the wrong idea.

"You know, our problems are far from over!" I said, shutting the Bible firmly. "I still find the whole thing very difficult. It might be more convenient to pretend, but I'm not going to."

"I wouldn't want you to, darling." I could tell he meant it.

"What I mean is, I'm still light years behind you in understanding and I've hardly started on the experience. I hear you all jabbering away in tongues down there and I want nothing to do with it. Then I get to church and you tell me we must live together as brothers, share everything! If God in His wisdom decided I was to be your wife, then He'll have to give you a lot of patience while I catch up."

It was just as well that the next meeting with Alan helped quite a bit in the catching-up process. I heard how much God loved me and that Jesus by dying on the cross took all my sin and my sinful nature upon himself. If was now possible for me to have a relationship with God—this was good news! It gave me a sense of much-needed security. The other side of the coin, which was what Alan tackled next, was that there was absolutely no way in which I could please God.

"The normal human thing to do is to justify yourself," Alan explained. "You set up your own standards of behavior, decide what you would like to achieve in a day, or a life-time, and if you get anywhere near that, you're happy. But that doesn't mean God is pleased with you."

Gradually I saw how many ways I had turned away from the life God wanted me to live. All that keeping Him at arm's length was not just time wasted, but rejection of God's love, which was sin. I fell into silence as I considered this, and looked down at the hands on my lap. For some minutes I let the realization dawn that Christ had died because I was a sinner, and began to see myself as I really was. I thought of myself as a failure in some ways, but I still thought I could do something about it, with a bit of effort. I looked beyond my hands to the pattern on the carpet, then to the overstuffed armchair in which I was sitting. A little further up and Alan's shoes came into view. They were still. He was waiting, I suppose. When I looked up properly he was sitting as though he were still listening, with his elbow resting on the corner of the chaotic desk-top and his chin held between his thumb and first finger, but his eyes were closed. He became aware I was looking at him and opened his eyes, smiling at me.

"I'm sorry, I was praying. Do you mind?"

Seeking God

"It seems to be the only thing to do, really." My voice was very low. I felt so unworthy of God's love.

We prayed together for a long time. Mostly it was me saying sorry to God for all the ways in which I had failed. Gradually the tone changed as Alan thanked God for His forgiveness and love, and I became aware what this meant in a new way, because I didn't deserve it.

"I think you have reached the stage of decision. Would you like to write a letter to Jesus?" This was the same idea that Colin found so helpful. It was a preparation for commitment which made it much more personal and thoughtful. I had two more weeks to think things through, but I knew already that I could at last say for myself, "Yes, I want Jesus to be Lord of my life."

Alan came to our house two weeks later, and we went into the church to pray together. I had spent so many church services on the back row. Now we knelt at the front. Alan put his hands on my head and we prayed together. I was full of expectation. I thought everyone came away from a time like this leaping and grinning and praying in tongues. For me it didn't happen like that, but I was not disappointed when I didn't pray in tongues. This was a secondary issue. The peace I felt was gift enough.

That Sunday worship was quite different. Colin's sermon actually made sense as well, although I realized as he spoke that he had been preaching in the same vein before, when it was like gibberish to me.

HIS GOD, MY GOD

"We are all familiar with the great commandments of love. 'You are to love God with all your heart, mind, soul and strength. And you are to love your neighbor as yourself.' We have learned how impossible it is to even attempt to keep those commandments in our own strength. We have also discovered that we do not have to depend upon our limited human resources of love. 'Your God has been pleased to pour the unlimited resources of His Holy Spirit into our hearts and lives. And that Holy Spirit of God is the Spirit of Love.' "

At last I felt I was on his wavelength, or perhaps it was God's wavelength. My mind could grasp this, it fitted together. As he moved on, however, I knew I still had a lot to learn.

"When He repeated to the disciples that the promised gift of the Holy Spirit would soon be given to them, Jesus completed the commandment of love. For there is a third part of His loving purpose in our lives. He said: 'A new commandment I give to you, that you love one another; even as I have loved you, that you also love one another.'

"Not only are we to love God and our neighbor; we are to love one another. The Lord repeated the commandment a little later: 'This is my commandment, that you love one another as I have loved you.' It seems impossible. How can we love each other in the way Jesus has loved us? And yet He was in no mood to play spiritual games with His disciples. He gave this new commandment on the night of His arrest and crucifixion. He meant what He said and in the very next verse He explains what He meant: 'Greater love has no man than this, that a man lay down his life for his friends.'

"That is how Jesus has loved us. He went to the cross for us. He lived for us, died for us, and was raised to life for us. He laid down His life for us. If we are to love one another in the same way, that means that God is saying we are to lay down our lives for one another.

"I believe this is the scripture that God is laying before us at this time. This week I asked Him what it means to lay down our lives for one another. And, friends, it means that we are to learn to live for one another, rather than ourselves, to realize we are part of this congregation for the sake of all the other members rather than for our own selfish motives. Each of us is a member of the Body of Christ, here to love one another, serve one another and live for one another."

As the months passed, Colin's sermons probed further and further in this direction. Gradually the congregation saw that they needed to express the love of Jesus for the world by their life together. More and more people crowded into the church, many of them with deep needs. Colin spent hour after hour with them, and some of them would stay and talk to me if he was busy.

"You know, all this doesn't make much sense," Colin sighed as he joined me in the kitchen after seeing someone to the door. "It's not good enough. We talk to poor Rosie there about loving acceptance in Christ, and then send her home to a family where it's 'every man for himself.' There are so many like her."

"Well, the only alternative to sending her home, is having her to stay here," I puzzled. "And that's not okay, is it?"

"Or is it?" Colin suddenly sounded more enthusiastic. "What have I been preaching about all this time? Perhaps we could help some people like that."

"But so few," I remonstrated. "How could we leave the others out?"

"That's where the church comes in. Between us we could shelter quite a few folk."

"But just a minute! Why should the rest of the church do anything of the kind? It is asking rather a lot."

"Oh, we couldn't do it all at once. At the moment, as you say, I have no right to suggest anything like that. But we can't expect others to do anything we don't."

We discussed these ideas on many occasions, always with the same conclusions. There were so many situations where the only way to offer Christ's love seemed to be to take someone away from a poisoned home environment. I understood enough about Christ's new love now to want to share it with others. It seemed that I could do this in a practical way by sharing the house, leaving the spiritual side to Colin.

Seeking God

I really believed in what he was doing and wanted to help. As this seemed to be the way forward, I wanted to be one with Colin this time.

But would my shallow-rooted faith stand the strain?

5

Help!

There was no doubt in my mind that it was right to have people living with us. Colin was sure that was what God wanted, I trusted Colin to know and understand God, and even in my own terms it made sense. However, three or four days were enough to show me that I was utterly unprepared and unequipped for the upheaval.

For the first few months there was Mary, who was separated from her husband. She came with her two sons aged eight and ten, and a "fostered" daughter. Along with the daughter came her boyfriend, who didn't officially live with us, but in practice often slept on the sofa. Between them they manifested a whole range of problems, emotional and psychological, social and moral.

Marrying Colin and setting up home with him was the only experience I had of sharing the practicalities of life and merging two routines. Now our life style was in constant chaos. We never knew how many would turn up for the next meal, or when the next angry outburst would take place.

HIS GOD, MY GOD

There seemed to be people in my house, my kitchen, all day long. Guests used to send me into a frenzy of cleaning, and now I was never free of them. To compensate, I withdrew into myself and became two people. One was coping quite well, always just about to get on top of the housework and talking freely to Mary about practicalities. The other was full of burning resentment against God for giving the idea to Colin in the first place, against Colin for allowing it to happen, against all these people for intruding into my life. The conflict between these two parts of myself was constant and exceedingly painful. I clenched my fists and battled on. Often, when the house was empty, I found myself crying from sheer fatique and frustration. I confided in no one. I was alone.

"Have you finished in the bathroom?" Mary's voice rang down the stairs.

"Coming!" I dropped the toys I was tidying, and went upstairs. A long-distance conversation would disturb the children, whom I had just got to bed. After bathing all three there was so much tucking up and story-telling that I had never got back to the bathroom.

"Just give me a couple of minutes. I'll turn on the water while I clean up, and you can go down and tell the boys to get ready. Their program finishes soon."

"O.K. Thanks." Mary disappeared.

So I was to have no latitude about the timing of cleaning the bath. We had both agreed that of course we would clear up when we finished. Mary was quite justified in summoning me. That didn't stop me

Help!

growling inwardly as I dropped to my knees and fished out the flannels.

I focused my mind on my negative reactions and hated myself. "I must stop. Relax." The side of the bath was cool on my forehead. "Remember to take down that dress to mend, remember to tell Colin about that phone call, remember to put dog food on the shopping list, don't forget . . . stop. Relax. No, concentrate, or you'll never get through. Oh, for goodness' sake!" I turned on the taps to remove the scummy high-tide mark, washed the bath in a fury of activity directed against myself and drove myself on again.

"Bathroom's clear." Poised and smiling, I stuck my head round the sitting room door. Immediately the battle began.

"Oh, Mum, can't we just stay until half past eight? I want to see the next program."

"No, Neil, I told you after this one."

"But Mum, it's all about genes like we're doing at school."

"Well, maybe . . . ."

I couldn't take any more, and closed the door. I'd have to turn the taps off, or there'd be a flood. Mary's disciplining of the boys was her problem!

The reasonable half of me stood by helpless while the other half fumed. In my mind I had always realized that there was bound to be friction when two households tried to live together. In my mind I had decided that it would be possible to overcome this, to understand that with twice as many people in the

HIS GOD, MY GOD

house there would be twice as many breakages, twice as much wear and tear. But my heart remained firmly closed to the reasonings of my mind, and resented it all terribly. Neither could my heart understand that my way might not be the only right way, and that other people were having to adjust to me as well as I to them. Why, when the whole idea had been put to me, had I only listened to my mind, and not taken my heart into consideration? If this state of affairs continued, I could divide into two permanently and have a nervous breakdown or something. I felt desperate.

Colin, my mainstay, was shut out of my conflict as firmly as anyone else. It was partly his fault, after all. He was out at some meeting—as usual. I could not even take him a cup of coffee, and share my worries with him. He would accept me, understand. But bother it. I would sort this out for myself. He would have all the answers, he would pray for me. Fat lot of good that had done in the past. Perhaps he was praying for me now. Why can't he keep God out of this? It's my life.

When he returned home I did make some coffee, and did tell him about the phone call, but was so short with him the coffee must have tasted very bitter. I shut the door firmly on him and left him to think whatever he wanted.

For six weeks I went through a form of self-inflicted hell. My sense of injury and injustice increased daily. Every hurt was jumped upon, stuffed to the back of my mind and left to fester. How hard done by I was! I was

Help!

like a badly-made firework, ready to go off at the sight of a spark.

The explosion came the day I found holes burnt by a cigarette through the sofa cover. Someone obviously felt guilty about it, because a cushion was lying nonchalantly over the spot, probably so they could get away and be out when I saw it.

I beat my fists against the sofa until my arms ached, then burst into tears, holding the cushion against me. I cried for a long time. There was some sense of release, but no peace. When they all returned I hardly spoke to them, especially those I suspected, but otherwise carried on as normal. Then, later in the evening, my control broke again, and Colin found me lying on our unmade bed, sobbing quietly.

"Darling." He just held me. Immediately I stiffened and reached out for another tissue. His hands dropped back to his knees. Sitting still, he waited for me to say something. I took a deep breath.

"I need to get away. I must think." Reams of emotion lay behind that, and Colin must have had so many questions, but he knew better than to ask them.

"Why don't you go and see Audrey?" He meant my stepmother, who lived an hour's drive away. "If you go tomorrow I can look after the children. It's my day off, and I've got nothing particular to do. You haven't seen her for ages. She's probably got no idea of what we're up to here."

I thought about it. Driving away, leaving it all behind me. For a moment it was such a heady feeling I toyed

HIS GOD, MY GOD

with the idea of not coming back. My emotions were always dragging me to extremes.

"You're right. And it would be good to just talk to her."

"All right, then, that's settled. Now don't you think it would be better if you came down and stopped sulking around up here?"

"Oh, Colin, I can't."

"Come on, it would do you good. You go and wash your face while I make the bed." I didn't move. It suddenly seemed important that I should get my own way. Why should I follow him? If I wanted to stay here and wallow, that was none of his business. Yet what would it achieve? What good was it to run away? Under all the resentment I still knew in my mind that in opening our house, Colin was doing God's will. He was putting up with as much inconvenience as I was, and my attitude was making it ten times worse for him. And now he was trying to help me escape tomorrow. I could show him no affection, but I could make this gesture of reconciliation.

Even that I did with a bad grace, as I heaved myself slowly off the bed and went out without a word. Yet for me it was a symbol. I would try again. This time I would win. I would explain it all to Audrey so that she would understand. I would convince her and myself at the same time that it was worth all the trouble, that obeying God was all that mattered.

Somehow it didn't quite turn out like that.

Help!

Because she didn't have a phone, I had contacted her at work to discover when she was off duty and met her outside the nursing home where she worked. As I saw her slim, energetic figure moving towards the car, I felt very affectionate towards her and was glad I had made the effort to come. We had grown very close several years previously, especially since my father died. It would be good to talk to her. I greeted her cheerfully, and it wasn't until we had driven out of the built-up area that she put two and two together.

"Caroline, you've got something on your mind. It must be serious or you'd have brought the children. What's it all about?"

"Well, yes, I do want to talk to you. Hang on."

I slowed down and pulled the Cortina into an open gateway. When the engine was still, I looked out across the field and took a deep breath.

"Well, it's like this . . . ."

Although I balked at explaining Colin's baptism in the Spirit, I sketched in the background by saying that Colin was now finding his work much more fulfilling and demanding, and that he could now see God working in everyday situations in a new way. I wasn't sure how clearly I was explaining the spiritual side of things, but Audrey knew what it was to help people. She could follow the reasoning behind long-term help for people such as those living with us, but could also see what pressure it was putting on me. My well-meaning aim of "bringing her up to date with what was happening" was a mark I could no longer hide behind.

HIS GOD, MY GOD

What I really wanted to do was to pour out all my confused feelings.

I realized I had said too much when I suddenly heard her commenting:

"Well, it looks as though it's gone too far to pull out now."

"But Audrey, I wasn't dragged into this. Colin had the idea first, but we've talked about it a lot, and I really wanted to give it a try. It's just that . . . oh, silly things really. My kitchen isn't my own. They use metal spoons in saucepans when I only use wooden ones, they never quite finish the washing up, so I have to go and do the dog's bowl, put out the milk bottles and things like that. Then, when I finally finish, I go into the sitting room and all the chairs are taken. I stood there for ten minutes the other night, and no one thought of squeezing up on the sofa to make room for me." I had been absent-mindedly fingering the steering wheel of the Cortina as I spoke, and this had become an agitated fiddling and then tightened into an angry grip. I stared out through the windscreen at the corn and tried to soothe my mind back into order. "I mean, we're trying to help them, and don't want anything in return, but that's a bit much."

"They do help you with the housework, though."

"Yes, of course. But . . . I haven't really had time to think about it much. It's all been on top of me. I think it's because they do everything differently. And it feels odd to know that someone else has ironed the shirt Colin is wearing."

Help!

"Can't imagine many wives complaining that someone has done their ironing!"

"It sounds silly when I say it."

"Don't worry. I do understand. But don't make mountains out of molehills. I've spent some time with a house full of people. You have to learn that you're probably upsetting their routine just as much, and they haven't got the security you've got, with a husband, and house, and all."

"There won't be much house left by the time they've finished with it."

"You're not so hard done by. If you feel this is what you both want to do, you must work through all the little problems together."

Although we talked all afternoon, exchanging gossip about the children and her friends, Audrey had pronounced her verdict, and that was that. Thinking about what she said as I drove back, I decided that I got what I deserved. It had done me some good to talk it all out, but the sober fact was that I had to return and make a go of it. Surely I could sort out these teething troubles.

It was many months before Colin was able to tell me what he had done that same day. He knew my turmoil. His understanding of it, which he could never have told me at the time, was that our prayer for my baptism in the Spirit was being answered. This was a time of cleansing, of bringing to the surface the many tensions which dominated my life. The old self was at war with the new person I was so afraid of becoming, and I was

HIS GOD, MY GOD

clinging on to my way of doing things, in fact, rebelling against God.

Analyzing it in this way didn't completely dissipate the pain he felt on seeing me suffer, and, as I suspected, he was praying constantly for knowledge about how to help me and for God to intervene and calm the storm.

As he prayed on that afternoon, God gave him a prophecy, which he wrote down and still carries in his Bible.

I will go before you in the matter of the community. There is nothing to fear. Simply be obedient to the leading of My Spirit. This was born in My mind so it will not fail. Now consider the days that lie ahead. They will be days of pain, of much traveling and yet they will be days of much success, for I will speak My words through your mouth and many shall hear and respond. Salvation shall come to many hearts.

Concerning your wife: know that she is as a bright jewel in My crown. Her sincerity of heart delights Me and I shall use her to point the way for many to My Kingdom. Your prayer to be united in My love has been heard and I make you this promise: As you remain faithful to Me, so shall I remain faithful to you, and your love for one another shall deepen, for the Son of

Help!

Righteousness shall fill your life together. As the sun draws out the different colors of creation, so shall the Son highlight your love for one another. You have much to learn together but I will be your teacher . . . .

So it was that when I returned home, we had both found peace where we had each looked for it. Mine, however, was not to last for long. While Mary and Sue were washing up, and I was making Clive's bed, a crash suddenly made me straighten my back. What had been broken now?

The old anger blazed again. Everything was made worse by having been away, not better. Yet once again I struggled with this wave of emotion, buried it and carried on. No one, not even Audrey, could help. I would have to cope alone.

For two more weeks I fed myself on resentment and self-pity. Then Colin had to go away for the parish weekend at which the Fisherfolk were ministering. They were a music group from Houston, Texas, who had recently started a community in England. I, of course, was left with the children—thank goodness!

That weekend Claire had a sore throat and everything seemed to go wrong. The hours seemed to drag by, and I had to make meals I didn't want and Claire couldn't eat. By Sunday night I was drained, not with the tiredness of healthy activity, but with boredom and grinding routine.

I was half-way up the stairs when I heard Colin and

HIS GOD, MY GOD

the team come back, laughing and obviously having a great time together. I knew the sort of report I would get if I asked.

"The Lord did wonderful things this weekend. We've had the most fantastic times of praise together." I would have hated to go, but that was not the point. Everyone else had a good time, gained victory over their problems, and I was stuck at home, never seeing an end to this struggle, and certainly not praising the Lord!

I couldn't bear to be polite to their smiling faces; Colin could try to drag me downstairs again if he wanted, I wasn't going to shift.

Once again I flung myself full length on the bed. I could go no further, fight no longer. I had no strength left. Someone else would have to cope.

Before I could stop myself, I heard myself crying out, like a hungry baby, who doesn't understand his pain.

"God, if You're there, You've got to help me. Show yourself to me because I can't take any more."

My sobs gradually quieted. I knew that God had done this and that He was there with me—at last.

6

In it Together

Very slowly, almost imperceptibly at first, my life began to change. I had come to the end of my own resources many times before, but had always relied on myself to get up and keep going, somehow. I could not admit to the world or to myself that Caroline Urquhart could not cope with her own life, however much of a mess it was. It was my life, and I wanted to be in control.

This time it was different. At last, for the first time, I had actually asked God to take over—and meant it. I would have been reluctant to call the incident "my conversion," because it was but one step in a whole chain of events, but from now on God became a conscious part of my thinking. I only now allowed Him to do what He had been longing to do, to draw the pain and confusion out of my life and give me His peace.

To begin with, I was aware that I had more control over the negative thoughts which had embittered relationships within the household. I had wallowed in self-pity, really quite enjoying it in a painful way. I had assumed others would let me down, and was almost pleased when they did. Slowly I recognized that my inferiority complex and sense of rejection had hardened until they became a point of pride, a barrier I could hide behind. Facing up to this new understanding of myself took a great deal of courage, but as the tight knots of hatred were untangled, life became bearable again. Not that I believed I had come to grips with my life: the principal lesson I had learned was that life with me at the helm was a miserable affair. Learning to put Christ first is a life-long process, but at least I had begun.

I hoped that people in the parish had been unaware of my struggles, as I had intended them to be. I had maintained a mask of self-sufficiency and of loyalty to Colin which I trusted to have satisfied the average outsider. Those who could read between the lines and were joining Colin in prayer for me also had the insight to keep quiet about it to me.

It was my relationship to Colin, therefore, which lay heaviest on my conscience as I emerged from my self-made pit of depression. I had turned a cold shoulder for too long, unable to accept affection. At first I thought I could convey my "apologies" by simply turning over a new leaf and relating to him normally again. Certainly he soon noticed the warmer greeting when he came in, the more open discussion of the frictions of community, and even, sometimes, laughter, which I had almost forgotten existed.

As time went on though, I felt increasingly that I

In it Together

needed to be more explicit, to actually talk it through with him. This wasn't easy, not only because of my having to "eat humble pie," but because we never seemed to be alone together except at the end of another exhausting day.

Then, one night, with everyone in bed and the sofa downstairs miraculously empty for once, Colin came in late but not tired. I was upstairs but waiting for him, and came down for a chat.

"Ah, this is good," sighed Colin, stretching his legs. "I wonder how long it is since we've had the place to ourselves." He looked at me and grinned. "Well, nearly anyway!"

"Does it get on top of you, sometimes? Like when you come home tired and Clive tearfully hands you the latest casualty among his toys to mend?"

"Oh, I can usually face coming home." He smiled slowly. "Especially now that I've got a new-style wife."

"What do you mean by that?" I asked, intrigued to find out what had impressed him.

"Well, I used to see a great deal more of your back than your face," he chuckled. "A great solid back standing at the sink, disappearing up the stairs, all over the place. It's good to hear you singing."

"Am I singing?" I hadn't realized that.

"You certainly are. Real songs of praise too!"

"I must have been an old misery. I'm so sorry." There, I'd said it. It wasn't that difficult, after all.

"I forgive you, my darling. But you know it wasn't me you were fighting. I was just grieved by the pain I saw in you, but I couldn't help. You insisted on finding your own way. No, the person you need to apologize to is the Lord. You need to repent of your rebellious spirit, if you haven't done so yet."

I gave a wry smile. "I thought I'd got off rather lightly."

"You have got off lightly. The Lord doesn't want to punish you for your rebellion: He wants to forgive you. You need to give yourself to Him in a new way and understand that He has already paid the price for you. He has suffered the punishment that you deserve."

I must have changed. I couldn't have sat there quietly and be preached at like that before. But what Colin was saying made sense now. I'd been feeling the need to clear up the past in some conscious way.

"I think you're right. It's God I need to talk to. I want to talk to you at the moment though, since I've got you to myself." There followed a long pause. Then I looked up to see Colin smiling quietly at me. I raised an eyebrow.

"Oh," he explained, "it's just that I'm amazed at your strength of will. You were living here in the center of spiritual renewal, listening to sermons that brought others to their knees in repentance, seeing God at work all around you, and yet you remained firmly untouched by all of it." His voice was teasing, and yet serious.

"Not so much of the untouched, if you please! All my traumas were the direct result of what was going on around me. I just ran away from it, instead of towards it like everyone else."

"Does it look so dreadful from outside?"

"No . . . well yes, sometimes. You'd think it would be easy to ask for healing, but that means admitting you can't do it yourself. Even though I don't have a particularly high opinion of myself, it's still a blow to pride, and pride, like you said from the pulpit on Sunday, is one of our big problems."

"So my sermons are not in vain!"

"Strangely enough, they were the only way you could get through to me. I would never have listened to you in conversation with me, as you understood. I just didn't want to know."

"You're telling me!" Although he was joking, I sensed again what a difficult time it had been for him.

"I suppose I'll never really know what it felt like, living with me. And you'll never really understand what I was going through," I mused quietly. Then I added firmly. "But from now on it's going to be different. We can share things as they happen. We can look at them the same way I've jumped over the fence now and become one of you. Who would have thought it?" I grinned. "One of them."

"Was I a 'them'?" Colin grinned back.

"Most certainly. You were 'Colin and that God of his'. Now your God is my God."

Colin heaved a great sigh. "I've known that for some while of course, but to hear you actually say it like that . . . I don't know whether to cry with relief or whoop with joy. Come here and . . . ."

But I was in his arms already.

"And our God wants to be everyone's God. Everyone from the tiny face in the back corner of the congregation to my own wife." He reached out for my hand. "Come on, wife. It's time we were in bed."

A few weeks later, Michael and Jeanne Harper visited our church to lead a conference.

Michael had founded the Fountain Trust, the aim of which was to promote renewal within the Church. The subject of his meetings was to be "The Baptism in the Holy Spirit": a subject that had made me wince in the past. Hadn't Colin prayed that I would be filled with the Spirit? Where was the evidence that God had answered this prayer? Although I could see that God was changing my life in some respects, I was still looking for an experience to confirm that I had been filled with the Spirit, because everyone else seemed to really know. I couldn't shake off my earlier conclusion that I was in some way unacceptable to God.

All of the old fears of inadequacy as a hostess swooped in on me at the prospect of meeting these people. Could I live up to their expectations, or would I let Colin down?

On the Friday night, Michael spoke in the church to the regular gathering of church members, and I was glad to give it a miss and look after the children. However, as the dutiful wife I had to free myself for the

In it Together

afternoon on Saturday to attend the open meeting which was being held in the school down the road. It was a sunny day, everyone seemed so expectant, and I felt dreadful. I went anyway. Did I really want something to happen to me? Did I want to pray in tongues? Part of me did, another part didn't. Certainly it would have been very difficult to take any public step of commitment even had I wanted to. The whole thing was acutely embarrassing; after all, I was the vicar's wife!

I suppose it was a good meeting. Everyone else seemed to think so. I spent the whole time writhing with frustration and self-consciousness, thoroughly miserable, and couldn't wait to get out. Wild horses wouldn't have got me to another meeting that weekend. I had done my bit, hadn't I?

When I got home at tea time Clive didn't feel like eating; he lay down on the sofa and I persuaded him to have a drink. He obviously wasn't at all well, so I put him to bed early. After midnight he crept into our room in the dark.

As soon as he climbed into bed, we knew something was horribly wrong. I had never felt such a temperature, and he was in a lot of pain. Sometimes I feel guilty about pestering doctors, but I didn't hesitate now.

When Colin came back from phoning he sat on his side of the bed and looked across the hot, prostrate body of Clive at me. Then he held out a hand and took mine, stroking back Clive's hair with the other. There were a few moments of a dreadful, heavy silence when neither of us dared to speak.

Then I heard, "Darling, will you pray with me, for Clive?" We had never really prayed together. It was a difficult question to ask and to answer.

"Yes, I . . . ." I started, then had to clear my throat. "It seems to be the only thing to do, doesn't it?"

"Yes," Colin agreed.

"Go on, then. You pray. I'm not very good at it yet."

Colin prayed for several minutes, and I found myself adding, "Yes, Lord," like people in the meetings, all self-consciousness gone. In this real situation, where my needs and wants were totally unimportant, I could come to the Lord with the right attitude of heart. We were united by more than the holding of hands as we pleaded for our son. The undercurrent of praise gradually swelled up within us both, and Colin started praying in tongues. I sat quietly, my heart no less involved for the silence.

"He's going to be all right, isn't he?" I looked to Colin for reassurance. I could see that he was quietly confident.

We didn't have to wait much longer for the doctor.

"I'm glad you called so quickly," she said, probing gently at Clive's side. "Acute appendicitis, I think. We must get him to the hospital straight away. Where's the phone?"

Others living in the house proved a great advantage under these circumstances, as it meant we could both go to the hospital and leave the girls asleep. Colin

In it Together

drove the car carefully through the wet empty streets of the small hours of the morning, while I held Clive wrapped in blankets. He seemed so hot and, although the hospital was very close to us, the drive there seemed to take twice as long as usual. I felt as if it were all a nightmare, but confident that God had heard our prayers. The doctor in charge of admissions, after examining Clive, agreed he needed to be operated on immediately. After the decision was made, it seemed a peace settled upon Clive and he felt less hot.

Colin was chaplain to the hospital and was able to accompany Clive to the operating theater. He then suggested that we go home to get some sleep. Clive was in the Lord's hands, so there was nothing to fear. It was pointless to hang around at the hospital; Clive would not be conscious again until the morning.

I fell asleep as soon as I lay down, oblivious to everything until the waking household disturbed me. As soon as we had arrived home, Colin had been called back to the hospital in his official capacity as chaplain. It had been quite a night for him, but he had taken the opportunity to see Clive following the operation. He had been sleeping peacefully, and all was well: we could visit him later on in the afternoon.

It was good to hear this, to be assured that God had looked after every detail, and to know too that I had shared in the praying, at last! I hadn't expected a great miracle, but I knew our prayers had been answered. The Lord had given all three of us peace and allowed Clive to suffer for only a short time.

HIS GOD, MY GOD

Clive was allowed home four days later on the Wednesday, which was earlier than normal hospital procedure. He had made such a remarkable recovery that he felt able to do anything. I spent most of his period of "convalescence" trying to stop him riding his tricycle!

Increasingly now, I could examine events in my life and see that through them the Lord was teaching me the basic lessons of faith. I was a long way behind Colin, but I was following him rather than fighting. Although I was still not speaking in tongues myself, at least hearing others do so no longer disturbed me.

Because I was now more open to receiving God's help and His peace, I was much easier to live with. My acceptance of myself meant that I could accept others more easily, and where there were problems I just asked God for His love, instead of straining to manufacture it within myself.

Another tension in my life was dispelled as I saw that I needed to give Colin back to God, so that he could follow Him without fear of upsetting me. Before I had seen only a full diary, earnest conversations I resented, and a husband exhausted by the demands made on him. Now I could share in the glorious picture of people being released from pain, hatred, and confusion, as I had been. I joined one of the prayer groups which met every week. I could now rejoice with others as the news of healings of both mind and body were regularly received.

The outward circumstances of my life, however,

In it Together

were still much the same and fairly hectic. Our extended household was being extended even further. A homeless family who hoped to move into the parish stayed with us while looking for accommodation, and remained for nearly a year. This strained our resources of space, money and love quite a bit; but it was a situation Colin and I faced together and in God's strength, so had nothing like the effect of the first onslaught. At the same time, things did become rather chaotic, and the parish was rather alarmed to realize what "laying down their lives for each other" might mean. For the most part people supported us in prayer and awaited developments on the sidelines. It was about a year before others began opening their houses, especially to the many needy people who gravitated towards St. Hugh's.

Perhaps our household more than others was seen as a good place to go to talk things out, or just find company. Even if Colin was unavailable, people knew that I was usually in the house. Often while working in the kitchen, I would be listening or talking to those who had just dropped in for a chat! I didn't see this as a "ministry of counseling," or give it any label, but I was more than happy to talk to one man who often called in during his dinner hour, or give a cup of tea to one lonely person called Ray, who just seemed to want to sit. In this way, I somehow felt included in the total work of the parish, and began to gain a sense of identity and purpose. I found it difficult to accept that God had chosen me to be Colin's wife, but the idea fell

HIS GOD, MY GOD

a little more into place when I stopped resisting with all my might the love and life God had for me.

In any journey there are points from which one can look back and see how far one has come. One of these was reached for me the day that Betty stopped by and in the course of one of the conversations which had helped me so much, said, "Of course, I don't need to tell you how much you've changed."

"I'm never sure how much shows on the outside, but I know it feels different."

"Oh, you're a great encouragement to those of us who have been praying for you."

"How long has that been going on for?" I asked, amused.

"Longer than you would want to know about," she answered. "Long before you were prepared to give God a chance, we were praying."

"Well, if you and your friends are responsible for me being a Christian," I reasoned with a grin, "I hope you're going to keep on praying. I need it. Sometimes things get out of hand here, I feel I've had enough, and want to give up again."

"I can imagine that," grimaced Betty, "but you're still here."

"So you just keep praying, O.K.?"

7
Moving on

Before the year was out, we began to understand that this time of turmoil had served its purpose, and that the Lord was telling us it needed to come to an end. We had been quite sure that it was right to open our door, but had been unprepared for the way in which broken people had poured in until the house was bursting. The needs were overwhelming, and in ourselves we had felt totally incapable of meeting them. Still, we had been sent these people in particular to love, and we had set about our task with a will.

Gradually, we had begun to love and to give from more generous hearts. As valuable as this experience might be, however, we couldn't have continued to live with the strain our household was putting on us as individuals, as a couple or as a family.

Change was in the air. It was quite obvious what the Lord was saying and so we redoubled our effects towards finding accommodation for the other families, which in theory at least had been our aim for some time. When it came to the point it was hard to see everybody go. We had shared so much together that a bond had grown between us all. In answer to our concern, God continued to assure us that He would care for them in His way. By the time we came back from our summer holidays that year, we were ready to take a deep breath and start again.

The Lord showed Colin that a new household was to come into being. Whereas the first one had been based on the needs of the people in it, the second would consist of a mixture of people only some of whom would be classified as needy. We had learned much about God, and how He could care through us for others. On the other hand I felt I had failed to trust God enough to do this effectively. I sighed with relief that the past was over, and looked to the future with renewed understanding of my need for God.

Around the same time as the arrival of the second family, John had become a frequent visitor. Every now and again he would stay for a few nights, sometimes for quite extended periods. He obviously felt accepted by us, but never reckoned he really belonged. For him, the changes spelled decision. He had to face the idea of committing himself more fully to the household, or leaving us. Since making this kind of decision was one of the things in life John found most difficult, it was a great step forward when he announced that he wanted to stay.

Jeanne, who had been with us for several months already, also made a conscious decision to stay working in the parish full time. Everybody in this new

Moving on

household was convinced that God wanted them there. At the end of that summer, three such people arrived: Val, who was already in full time parish work, and Colin and Chris, who, like John, had jobs outside but were fully committed to the life of the household and the parish.

In addition several others came for a short period of time to receive ministry and healing. We responded to human situations as there was need, and those needs seemed to be unexpected and quite unpredictable in timing. Each change was significant, because we were learning to hear what God was saying to specific situations, and watching others and ourselves growing in grace and love.

Chris arrived on our doorstep, homeless, with a bulging suitcase and a heart full of bitterness and despair. The house was already full, and I didn't see that I could love anybody else, but as we stood at the door my heart was flooded with love from Jesus for him. He stayed for the weekend, then a little longer, then we all agreed that he should join us.

Now others in the parish opened their homes in this way. Some were based as we had been, on meeting people's needs; others lived together so that one or two of them were freed to work in the parish. Financially, all these households lived from a common fund, which enabled us to support several full time ministers in the parish. There were now so many spheres of work, groupings of people and activities needing to be co-ordinated, that it couldn't be a

HIS GOD, MY GOD

one-man job. Colin was grateful to be able to delegate different areas of his work to the people God was raising up to join him, and life settled down into a smoother routine.

The vicarage also became more peaceful and relaxed. This is not to say it was less busy. If anything, the change in atmosphere encouraged more and more people to drop in. It was an exciting time, and I was caught up in it.

One morning I had just returned from the mid-morning communion service when June rang the bell. I was pleased to see her, and rather surprised. She had been filled with the Spirit some months previously, but hadn't been around for several weeks, either in church or any other meetings.

"How nice to see you, June. Do come in." She returned my smile warmly, and I was relieved to find her so open. I thought she might have been rather on her guard, feeling guilty about her prolonged absence.

"I'm just having a coffee, June. Will you join me?" I stepped back into the hall, opening the door wider, but she shook her head.

"No, thank you very much. It's really Colin I've come to see. He's expecting me about now. Is he in the church?"

"Yes, he's not back from the service yet. I should go on over."

"O.K." June looked bashful, then took a deep breath. "You see," she confided, "I want to turn back to Jesus."

Moving on

"That's great, June," I enthused, as my heart gave a little hop and skip.

"Yes. Somehow I seemed to be side-tracked, and lost sight of the Lord. I was fairly happy with my life for a while, but then I realized I didn't have any peace like I'd had when I first became a Christian. So I'm coming back to ask God to forgive me and to make a new start. Do you know what I mean?"

She seemed nervous but was obviously full of expectation for this meeting. How well I remembered the anticipation when I had prayed with Colin, then with Alan, for God to fill me with His Spirit. I could share in June's excitement. It was an important day for her.

"Oh, I know exactly what you mean. I'm very happy for you." I gave her a quick hug. "I won't hold you up any more. You go and find Colin, and if you want a cup of coffee afterwards, you know where to come . . . ."

She went off down the drive, but my mind stayed as full of her as if she were still there. As I washed up, peeled vegetables and made beds, I prayed and prayed that God would meet her in the way she most needed. I was so thrilled that she had come back, and felt full of praise to God when suddenly, standing at the sink, I found myself singing in tongues! For several minutes I went on thanking God in this way, then fell into a companionable silence with Him. I could hardly believe what I was doing, and couldn't wait to tell Colin. Although I believed that I had already been filled with the Holy Spirit because of the changes in my life, I had

HIS GOD, MY GOD

long since given up asking for the gift of tongues. It is not an evitable result of being filled with the Spirit, and I thought the Lord simply didn't want me to have this gift. Now I was so surprised and excited.

Colin came back alone. He beamed through the window on his way to the door and I met him in the hall with an enormous hug.

"Was it a good time with June?" I asked into his ear.

"It was beautiful, praise the Lord," he answered into mine. "But I feel as though I've been missing something going on here as well." He held me at arm's length and looked me straight in the eye, appraisingly. I suddenly felt self-conscious and turned away.

"Actually, I've just sung in the Spirit," I tossed over my shoulder as I moved away. "Would you like a coffee?"

"Really?" He followed me. "And yes, please."

"Yes," I assured him, feeling safer where it had happened before, in the kitchen. "Listen."

And I couldn't. I was overcome with embarrassment until Colin started smiling at me, and we both ended up laughing with joy.

Over the next few weeks I began singing in tongues at home and in the service. A new sense of praise to God welled up within me. Any remaining fears about being unacceptable to God were swept aside and the sun seemed to have come out fully. I also found great strength in the fact that although I was often lost for what to say when praying for others, God could give me the words, and I knew I was praying effectively for

Moving on

them. The very issue which had caused me so much pain in the past was now a great source of joy.

The next year was a time of tremendous growth for the whole church. A deeper sense of fellowship was experienced by many people, who felt the Lord was calling them to share their lives and their resources. Fellowship groups were drawn together to make this possible, more and more hearts were opened, and more homes along with them. New friendships were established and strengthened.

I began to visit Norma, with whom Colin had spent so many hours praying for healing. She was moving freely now, without pain, and was a walking illustration to the church of the Lord's healing power.

Once a week, while the children were at school, we met to talk and pray together. It was good to have the opportunity to share some of the things that were going on in me and to pray about them.

Within our household we were experiencing Christian fellowship in a way which had not been possible with our previous extended family. Living so close to others teaches all concerned a great deal about themselves, some of which they may prefer not to learn. Judgmental attitudes can creep in all too easily, and we had to see for ourselves that where there is tension in a relationship, everyone involved needs to examine their attitude and be prepared to repent, even if it appears that the "fault" lies with one party.

Another thing I learned by living with others, which I

shared with Norma, was that it was just as important for me to receive others' help and love as to give it. If I couldn't, I was denying them the opportunity to give, and so blocking their spiritual development. It was also a mistake to think that Colin and I were giving the others a roof over their heads. That house belonged to the Lord, and was His to use as He directed. If ever I winced at a cup being broken, or mourned the wear of the carpet, I needed to remind myself that it wasn't mine in the first place. Every item, whether bought with Colin's salary, or a gift from personal friends, had to be "released" to the Lord. Sometimes this was painful, but it was necessary preparation for the future, as I came to recognize later.

For the single person there is much to be said for being accepted into a family, and the benefits are mutual. There is a price to be paid, however, when marrieds and singles are mixed. I found myself resenting Val. Only much later did I realize it was jealousy. She seemed freer than me of worldly concerns such as what the children could wear tomorrow, and hence more spiritual. She had a very effective role in the parish meeting pastoral needs, and even though I wouldn't necessarily have wanted to do this, I didn't myself have a clear-cut "spiritual" role, and felt second rate as a result. Many visitors called to see her, and I sometimes slid into the background to such an extent that outsiders mistook her for Colin's wife.

The kind of situation can be lived with for a while, but if it isn't brought out into the open, much pain can

Moving on

result. For me, it dragged up the old question of why God had chosen me to be Colin's wife. Did He wish I were more "spiritual"? From Colin himself I got nothing but reassurance, but even having dismissed this thought, I had to face my jealousy. I could comfort myself with the thought that those who were so free might be equally jealous of married status and my children. By reasoning I could cut the emotions of the situation down to manageable proportions, but it was second-best. It was many months before I was fully released, when I acknowledged the sin of jealousy and received forgiveness from the Lord.

I also had to grapple with the fact that the man I had married was fast becoming somebody of importance and was much in demand. The trickle of visitors from neighboring areas had become streams from a much wider area. Invitations to speak on missions, parish weekends, mid-week prayer meetings, Saturday praise meetings, Sunday services and conferences; week by week the requests came in and had to be dealt with.

As Colin saw the power of God working in so many lives, he was growing in faith all the time. Now that I was trying to understand more and more of God's will, I could more fully appreciate how far he was ahead of me. I just wasn't in the same league. While I spent all my prayer time trying to push out of my mind things like shopping lists and was there anything interesting I could do with cold lamb, Colin prayed with a notebook open in front of him, so expectant was he that the Lord would have something to say. When it came to guidance, I just left it to him. I had seen enough of his leading working out in practice to follow quite happily most of the time. When I felt that what he was doing or saying wasn't quite right, I would discuss my lack of peace with him and we always ended up agreeing as the Lord guided us together. But I left the decisions to him.

Yet with Colin accepting more and more speaking engagements, many decisions had to be made in his absence, and often there was only me to handle them. This was difficult as it had always been a weakness of mine to depend on others. Yet slowly, sometimes painfully, I learned to make a decision, carry it through without a frenzy of doubts paralyzing me, and defend it if it didn't quite work out. The next stage was being able to admit to myself and to others that I probably hadn't done the right thing without feeling that I couldn't look myself in the face.

During 1974 it was suggested to Colin that so many more people could benefit from the experience of his church if he would write a book. Trying to fit this unaccustomed discipline into his busy schedule seemed impossible, but every now and again he would wave a few sheets of paper at me. When I read these snippets it was nearly always with a view to the way he had brought in the various people I knew. Later I realized how much teaching he had crammed into the same pages. *When the Spirit Comes* was published in November of that year with the inevitable result that the speaking invitations which were already streaming

Moving on

in increased even more. This was no surprise to Colin.

"I really don't see how you're going to cope with it all," I confided to him in a rare quiet moment after lunch one day. "Looking after the parish is a full time job even with all the help you have. How can you travel more and still give the parish all the time and attention it needs? You're always tired as it is."

"You're quite right, darling. So where do I cut down?"

I puzzled over this for a while. "I suppose you could get more help in the parish, refuse even more of the invitations . . . ."

"But you know I've made that decision several times, and it isn't really a decision at all. The same problems remain. I'm finally coming to terms with what I know the Lord has been saying for a long time."

"What do you mean?"

"The possibility I've had to face is that we are being called away from St. Hugh's altogether, although . . . ."

I cut him short. "We can't do that. It's your job, your salary. Without it we've got nowhere to live. The children are happy at school here. And I'm happy . . ." I tailed off.

Colin leaned over and took my hands. "Don't think I haven't thought about it. It's not going to be easy, but I believe that's what the Lord is saying. I haven't told anyone else yet. I wanted you to have time to think and pray about it."

Leave! Leave St. Hugh's! The thought appalled me, dogged my thoughts all day long. Of course I had

HIS GOD, MY GOD

known that we would have to go some time, but surely not yet. I was only just beginning to grow as a Christian, and the thought of living without the parish community seemed impossible.

Despite our hesitations, we both reached the point where we knew that this was God's will, and approached the church leaders with the idea. At last, I could discuss it with Norma. I understood better now what God was doing, but I still had to deal with my emotions on the subject.

"At first, I didn't think it made sense at all," I said to Norma. She had probably been as surprised as the rest of the church when Colin had submitted the idea of our move to them at the Annual Meeting. Now she was interested to learn firsthand more of the thinking behind it.

"I don't really see how you're going to live," she said with a puzzled frown.

"Well, we're not exactly new to the idea of living by faith, are we? I mean, not having a salary is a big change, but in our first household we were always finding that we could feed ourselves on sums that at first sight were impossibly small. Above all, our faith has grown to the point where we trust God to provide even when we can't imagine how."

"What about a house?"

"That's a good example. I haven't got a clue how He's going to do it, but since I know this is the next step for us, I just know that one will turn up."

Moving on

Norma leaned forward. "Are you quite excited about it then?"

I thought for a moment. My reservations were being broken down, but that didn't mean I was going overboard yet.

"Yes and no. I love the people here. They have helped me through very difficult times before I became a Christian and with their care I have been well launched on my Christian life. I've never been happier. I suppose the place where you first meet with God is always special."

"It won't be the same without you, you know." Norma looked serious.

"So what is the general reaction in the church?"

"Well, everyone senses that this is what God is saying, but they don't want to face the implications of it."

"It is rather difficult to take in at first," I admitted, "but I'm sure this is right. I don't know how I'm going to cope without all the support I've grown used to, but obviously we have to face what the Lord is saying."

"Could you not still be part of the parish without Colin being vicar?" Norma's eyebrows were raised hopefully.

I sighed. This very question was one I was still not sure about. I was longing to stay, and this solution seemed perfect.

"I don't know, Norma. Would it work? That's one of the things we need to pray about this morning."

"Right then, let's start."

HIS GOD, MY GOD

I derived much strength from my times with Norma, and she played a great part in helping me to adjust to the idea of moving when we were firmly convinced that staying was not right. Again and again both Colin and I were being affirmed in our decision by prophecies, by Scripture, and by a peace that ran deeper than the surface objections. We didn't know how to go about establishing an itinerant preaching ministry, but Colin had an increasing vision of how the many invitations to speak could be formed into a coherent work.

This was just as well because, as time passed, the church began to have doubts as they realized what losing Colin would mean to their corporate life. These were relayed back to us, and we had to really pray the whole issue through again. Colin went to the bishop and was assured of his support at all times.

The crunch came when Colin finally signed the Deed of Resignation, which was irrevocable. We agreed to move after Christmas and a house belonging to the Fountain Trust was made available to us in East Molesey in Surrey. Vivienne de Pemberton and David Abbott were to come with us to support Colin in the practical and back-up aspects of his ministry. Now he would be free of parish duties and could concentrate on preaching the need for renewal in churches all over the country.

As the time to leave drew near, despite a growing excitement, I felt sad and lonely already in some ways. Through all that had happened to me, the Lord had been preparing me for a new depth of launching out in

Moving on

faith, but for some reason I found it much easier to trust God for the financial aspect than for my emotional needs. I was also worried about the children whom we were taking from a good church and from their school friends who were very important to them.

It was agreed between us all that we would leave on a note not of despondency, but of praise. Maintaining this attitude helped me a lot in the last few weeks. I didn't allow myself to think, "Poor me," let alone say it to others. The last four Sunday evening services were evangelistic, looking firmly to the future. In the parish communion on the last Sunday we were all sent out with members of the church laying hands on us: this was a difficult moment emotionally, but very uplifting. Despite having known so far in advance that we were going, the end came very quickly. Norma, Betty and so many others became part of our past. The future was largely unknown, but we did know that our sovereign and loving heavenly Father had planned every detail and would be there with us.

8

Living With God—First Class!

It was drizzling hard as we bundled out of the car. I locked all the doors as fast as I could, but this still gave Clive enough time to find a puddle. The aim of the game was to kick selected pieces of gravel cleanly over the top to land on the other side. I knew this because he often whiled away a spare moment in this way, but from the state of his shoes you would never have guessed he was trying to miss the puddle.

"Come on, Clive, we're going to be late!" Claire and Andrea had set off towards the church, and I hurried to catch up to them. Clive sprinted past me and ground to a brake-screeching halt just behind them. Somehow we arrived at the door together. Strains of a hymn rather more ancient than modern greeted us as I edged the door open and tried to slip in unobtrusively. By the time I had found the relevant page, the sparse congregation was on the last verse. I mentally abandoned the hymn and prayed that this time of worship would bring me closer to the Lord.

HIS GOD, MY GOD

We had been in East Molesey about two months. My worst fears had been confirmed. I quite enjoyed the jigsaw of fitting our furniture into a different house and planning where to put everything in the kitchen, but even when I'd finished all that, I didn't feel at home.

It wasn't the house's fault, I decided eventually. It was the lack of people. Not that a household of seven left a house empty, but we had lost the people who popped in, who phoned—in a word, the parish. Never was this more apparent than on Sunday mornings.

In my mind's eye I saw the clean, fresh lines of St. Hugh's, the white contrasting with the colorful splash of light from the stained glass, the packed congregation praising God with outstretched arms, eyes closed in contemplation of the great love shown in Jesus. Now I looked around me at the dreary gray walls and rows and rows of empty pews with a few people scattered around.

Just then Andrea tugged at my sleeve, and I bent down to catch her whisper.

"Why don't they sing, Mummy? Don't they love Jesus?"

Something in me snapped. I was finding it difficult enough to participate, so how could I expect the children to adapt to this when all they had ever known was St. Hugh's? They were now nine, eight and six.

By the time we had reached home and served up the lunch I had come to a decision.

"Next Sunday, we're going back to Luton for the day."

Living With God—First Class!

As Colin and the others would be away next weekend as well as this one, we would be able to go. I knew he would be delighted for us to have an outing.

Clive paused with the fork half-way to his mouth and said, "Oh, good," then carried on eating. Claire was more forthcoming.

"Oh, can we really, Mum? I could see Lorraine and Lisa again. That would be lovely."

Like Claire, there were many friends I wanted to see, and just being back among the church family at worship, with the freedom we had there, would be a real tonic.

Several times during the week that followed, the children made references to the forthcoming visit. As I tucked Claire into bed one night she said, "And tomorrow there will only be two days to go, won't there?" She didn't say what she was talking about, but I knew.

We had to get up quite early to be ready in time for the family communion, because it was over an hour's drive. Expectations were high as the children scrambled into the car and I checked mentally that we had all we needed. We were using David's Cortina, which I had often driven.

It was when we were overtaking on the motorway that the car started losing power. I know very little about cars. I pulled into the left-hand lane, glancing at the petrol gauge. No, that was all right. Something was definitely wrong though. Our speed had dropped, and the accelerator wasn't responding more than minimally.

HIS GOD, MY GOD

"Do you think we'd better pray, Mum?" This was Clive from the back seat, taking over as head of the household.

Without a moment's hesitation, all three began to pray together, out loud, Andrea singing in the Spirit over the top. I joined in.

As if the accelerator had just remembered what it was supposed to do, I felt the engine surge back to life. We hummed along again, our praises almost drowning the sound of the engine.

"Gosh, Mum, it worked!" Claire sounded as startled as I felt, and we all burst out laughing. We were still chatting away when the dragging sensation started again, as if a big hand were trying to hold us back. The children sensed it immediately.

"Let's pray again, Mummy," said Andrea. "It worked last time."

Again the car responded. From then on, we prayed our way every inch of that journey, and each time we stopped, we lost power. It seemed that it was getting worse between prayers. Five minutes before the service began we pulled into the drive of the friends we were going to spend the day with. By this time, the engine really sounded as though it were on its last legs, and when I switched it off, died with such a final sound that I thought it would never start again. As if we were abandoning a sinking ship, we piled out and hurried round the corner just in time for the first hymn.

It was marvelous to be there, to see so many friends

Living With God—First Class!

and faces we knew all around us, with their great smiles of welcome.

After a few minutes, however, I stopped feeling so bubbly. To begin with, I found it nearly as hard to worship as I had the previous week. Why should this be? This wasn't what I had expected. Neither of the curates was there and the sermon wasn't quite what I had been looking forward to.

"Lord, what are You trying to say to me?"

During the service, when I had expected to be completely carried along by the praise and worship, I felt detached. It was as if God was taking me on one side and rebuking me gently. Did I not believe that East Molesey was the place He wanted me to be? So I must accept that my church is now there, not here. I couldn't walk forwards into the life the Lord had prepared for me if I was forever looking over my shoulder. It was also wrong to look for God in certain places and people, when He was to be found in my heart, and that was where I should worship Him.

"I'm sorry, Lord. Please forgive me. You are always worthy to be praised."

The rest of the day was all we had hoped. We talked for hours, exchanging news of so many people. One member of the church who didn't even know us very well offered to have a look at the car, and grinned as he handed back the ignition keys.

"It should be fine now, but how you ever got here, I don't know. The distributor lead was broken. It's a miracle it ran at all."

HIS GOD, MY GOD

"Yes," I countered. "And it's just as much a miracle that you were around and free to mend the car. Thank you very much." My heart was singing. I had learned so much that morning, and a God who cared about every detail had brought us here just so I could hear what He wanted to say to me.

The next Sunday in church at home was quite different. In exactly the same surroundings, with the same congregation and very similar words to those which had left me cold, I found Jesus. I went expecting to be aware of Him and to hear Him speaking, and He did. The new understanding of Him living in me had released me to praise Him in a way I had never been able to before.

All the time we lived in East Molesey we very seldom had more than we needed, and would often see the money coming in at the last moment to meet the bills and provide our food. During the last days in Luton, it had seemed that the actual quantities of food had been stretched as we cooked and served it out; now it was the timing of the checks and money arriving which taught us again and again that our Father was a caring and generous God.

We had a lot to learn about other practicalities too. There was a great deal of administration to cope with and the team was totally inexperienced in planning an itinerant ministry. The biggest mistake was to leave too little time between trips to sort out the correspondence, do the long-term planning and fulfill all the other little duties of the average day. Somehow

Living With God—First Class!

the days allocated to relaxation were nibbled away to almost nothing because of little jobs which had spilled over. Then, before Colin, Viv and David had caught their breath, the next trip was upon them and the whirlwind began again: conferences, days of renewal, ministers' meetings, rallies and other services.

It wasn't long before the car, which always left bulging at the seams, showed signs of giving up the unequal struggle. We prayed about what we should be doing next, because although we might have enough to buy a reasonable second-hand car, there would be very little left over for other expenses. We had decided never to ask people for money, and wouldn't change that now. But none came as we prayed.

"I think we need to be more specific," said Colin. "Let's go and find the right car, find out how much we need, and ask for that." All sorts of problems leaped to my mind. How do you explain to a second-hand car salesman that you'll come back for the car when you've prayed in the cash? Somehow, Colin managed that part of it, and we started to pray for the amount needed.

"You know, it looks as though we're barking up the wrong tree," announced Colin. "At least, if I understood properly what the Lord was just saying to me."

"But how can we manage with an unreliable car?" puzzled David. "It's essential to the whole ministry." There were nods all around.

"I believe we should be asking not just for a car," expanded Colin, "but a new car so that it lasts." After

HIS GOD, MY GOD

thought, we all agreed. We prayed again. Colin went with David to choose the model, and came back to tell us how much money we needed.

"We've got a week to pay, and if we haven't got it by then, I've signed a hire purchase agreement in case."

"You what?" I exclaimed incredulously. "We'd better pray we don't need that."

The next day began a flow of checks, some big, some smaller. Some were from people we knew, with letters, others were anonymous. We reached the total the day before we were to collect the car. So much for the hire purchase! Even then, more money came in, so that we didn't have to drain the bank account of its few resources. We were thrilled, not because of the money, but because of seeing the Lord so clearly at work in our lives and the lives of those who sent the money. Our hearts were overflowing with praise and thanks to God. Another important lesson was there: the Lord doesn't want second best for His children. We needed to hear this one many times more, but our faith was stretched and strengthened every time we thought back on this provision.

Although there were times like this, of great excitement, I also knew what it was to have my heart in my boots. My emotions were not in the least reliable. I was very often lonely, and while I knew that worship was something that happened in the heart, it was uphill work praising in isolation from a worshiping body. In the low moments, I would feel that I had stopped growing spiritually. My faith, although firm, seemed to be static.

For a few days at a time I would see my prayers being answered, my decisions being confirmed, and everything would be marvelous. Then suddenly it would all go wrong: I would lose any confidence that the Lord was guiding me and make disastrous mistakes. My dejection grew each time this happened.

Then one day the Lord gave me the picture of a staircase. *"If you're going to be ready for the time ahead,"* He seemed to be saying, *"you've got a long climb to do in a short time. The trouble is that you learn one lesson well, but you don't keep moving. You're so excited about the previous step, you take your eyes off the next step and fall over it. Don't rejoice only at the progress you've made. Look up, look forward, and rejoice at what lies ahead, because I am your teacher."*

When we moved from Luton, many of our friends there and elsewhere expressed the fact that they would like to hear our news from time to time so they could pray for us. Although we wrote to as many as possible, a duplicated sheet was produced regularly and sent to committed prayer partners all the time we were in Molesey. Usually, Colin would write this, although Viv took over once or twice when Colin had long periods away. Most of the letter would be taken up with the news of the ministry, sharing how God was working in power, and many lives were made whole again, and physical ailments healed, as people

HIS GOD, MY GOD

responded to God's promises. It was very uplifting to sum up a few months' work and realize just how many things there were to praise God for. Sometimes the problem was estimating exactly what had been going on in a meeting, because Colin often left when it finished, and never learned in detail what the Lord had done. Some people did write of course, which was a great encouragement.

As I wrote my own personal letters, the fact was highlighted that all my friends were too far away to call on easily. I missed them very much. When Colin and the others were around it wasn't so bad; but when they had all gone off on some trip, life could be bleak. Here again, the Lord showed me that He cared.

We had been in East Molesey for about six months when Colin returned from a Fountain Trust conference with a most welcome piece of news.

"I think we've been sent a couple of friends. There was a retired brigadier at the conference called George Hoerder, a lovely man. His wife is called Hazel."

"But where do they live? What we need is someone practically on the doorstep."

"Well, how does round the corner suit you?"

"Oh, that's amazing. How long have they been there?"

"Moved just after us, and have been looking for people of a like mind ever since. You could have knocked us both over with a feather when we swapped addresses."

"It's fantastic. Is there anything the Lord can't do?"

Living With God—First Class!

"It doesn't look like it. I've invited them for lunch on Thursday, is that O.K.?"

Once George and Hazel had come into our lives, it seemed impossible that we had managed without them. George helped with the administration and soon became indispensable. Hazel had the knack of just loving people, and was always full of faith-building stories about the way the Lord was working. They were our main local source of fellowship. I wasn't alone any more. There was someone to call in on, someone who turned up on my doorstep in the middle of the morning, instead of the busy but empty hours stretching predictably ahead of me until the children returned.

With Colin away so much, however, there were many times when the final responsibility had to fall on me. I had to learn to be both mother and father to the children. My growing ability to make decisions was stretched even further under these conditions. Prayer became a matter of great importance, and instead of following Colin I learned to expect the Lord to speak to me more directly. A big step in this was taken during a period of ten days alone, when I was sharing my need of support with the Lord. In Isaiah 54:5, I read:

> For your Maker is your husband—
> The Lord Almighty is his name—
> And the Holy One of Israel is your Redeemer,
> He is called the God of all the earth.

HIS GOD, MY GOD

What more could I ask for? This was even better than having Colin at home all the time would have been. My heavenly husband was there, and since God was my Maker, He would know my needs better than I knew them myself. Hadn't He proved He could meet them?

Not long afterwards, Colin left for Australia and New Zealand for seven weeks. This really put my faith to the test. My new understanding that the Lord was my husband sustained me in many little incidents, but towards the end of that time, an unexpected bill came in. Colin had left enough in the bank to cover all he had anticipated, but suddenly here was another three hundred and fifty pounds to find! Viv, David and I prayed together: this was the first time we had asked for so much at one time without Colin. None of us, if asked, would have said that that made any difference, but it was a tremendous boost when the money arrived, in time, and before Colin had even heard of the dilemma. So the Lord really was our God, as well as Colin's.

When Colin returned, my confidence had been greatly increased, and I had my hands firmly on the reins. Now I would have to learn to hand them back. I hadn't anticipated any problem about that, but there was more adjustment needed than I had bargained for.

Still, my new confidence was a good and necessary development. Colin, on the other hand, had become almost self-contained. This had been essential to see him through so many weeks on his own, with the tremendous demands of an intensive ministry, but it was no asset to harmonious family life. He found it difficult to relate to us, and almost seemed not to need us. This was something we needed to treat seriously, work at together and make allowances for, each time he returned from a long spell away.

Step by step we were growing. The Lord never pushed us too far, or too fast, and He compensated for our weaknesses so that even in failure, we were being built up for His work.

9
The Hyde

"Lord, you've heard all our discussion about whether it's right to ask for a boat. We praise You daily for the food we eat and the necessary bills which are paid by Your provision, but we hesitate to ask You for something which we want for our own pleasure. Yet You taught man from the beginning that he needs times of rest and relaxation. Lord, I believe You want us to have a boat, so I pray that You will send us three hundred pounds tomorrow."

I had often been surprised by the audacity of Colin's prayers but this time I was still in a state of shock when we finished our household time of prayer.

"What made you pray that?" I asked bluntly. "We've been thinking about it for long enough, but I didn't know you'd reached a conclusion."

"Until I spoke that prayer, I didn't either," he said with an impish grin.

"Well, at least we're not going to be in suspense for long," I laughed. "You've really put in a tall order there if you expect the answer by tomorrow!"

HIS GOD, MY GOD

Next morning, a check for exactly £300 arrived.

"You must have been told it was coming," I teased, but I knew Colin was almost as surprised as I was.

"Are we actually going to spend it on a boat then?" he pondered incredulously. We were still not happy about spending money on ourselves, even though it seemed clear that the Lord had supplied this particular gift for such a purpose. We still had much to learn about His generosity. It was several months before we were finally convinced that we were free to spend the money in this way, but we spent many glorious hours that summer and for years after splashing up and down the Thames in the little fiberglass sailing boat. The importance of relaxation was something we were to underestimate time and time again, but this boat was a visible reminder that the Lord sees us as complete people, not just units from which He wants the maximum amount of work.

In January 1977, leaving the family in the care of a friend and Viv and David, I went on my first long trip with Colin and was given a closer look at the kind of demand made on him. He had been invited to give a week's Bible exposition at Haldon Court in Devon.

At the end of the second day, I closed the door of our room with a sigh and stretched out on the bed. Colin sat beside me and took my hand.

"Tired, darling?"

"Mm," I paused. "It always seems to be such a struggle to get to know people. I hate going through

The Hyde

the 'Where do you come from?' stage. I never know where to start."

"You're doing very well. From what I heard of your conversation with the lady in the pink trousers—Sheila is she called?—you seemed to be getting through."

"Oh, maybe." I was reluctant, as always, to accept his encouragement.

"Above all, to look at you as I talk, smiling quietly in the front row, and know that you are praying home every word to somebody's heart, that is all the support I need. I don't wonder you're tired. You've been praying for the better part of four hours since tea."

"But you've had to talk, pray and counsel all that time as well."

"I'll survive," Colin smiled, and the bed creaked under him as he crossed his legs. "In some ways, this week is quite a change for me. Lately I seem to have specialized in one-night stands with massive numbers. You never get close to anybody like that. It's exhilarating, of course, but in this sort of situation I can teach in greater depth and follow up themes."

I understood also, by the end of the week, how faith is fed by being constantly dependent on the Lord while ministering. So often your own resources of strength, of love, of sensitivity, are inadequate. It is essential to hear what the Lord is saying in specific situations, and to learn the necessity of obedience.

Obedience for me often took the form of accepting the consequences of Colin's obedience. Each step forward meant a change in him which I had to adjust,

HIS GOD, MY GOD

and Colin never seemed to stop for rest. Perhaps the most difficult thing was that when really deep changes were going on, they were often painful and confusing times for him and he wasn't able to share them until afterwards, or at least until he understood what was going on himself. He would withdraw from me. To perfectly straightforward comments I would get vague answers, like from someone who is reading the paper and doesn't want to be disturbed. I had to learn that he wasn't uninterested but that his attention was focused elsewhere. At such moments, especially if I needed some kind of support, I resented his obedience. Effectively I was saying to the Lord, "But Lord, I've only just got used to the last change. Can't we have a bit of rest?" Repenting of this attitude was one of the most difficult forms of obedience the Lord asked of me, but one that I knew was important. Colin should not feel under pressure from my reactions or expectations, but be free to follow the Lord. At such times the Lord would lovingly remind me that He himself was my husband and would meet all my needs.

Soon after that, there was a tour of South Africa which was for Colin the most amazing and draining trip so far. After it he was not in the least spiritually dry, but he was in a state of physical exhaustion which was the result not only of that one trip, but of all the previous months of overdoing it and never quite catching up with the administration. George, who had been helping out to a certain extent in the past, now formally took over the reins of this aspect of the work, with Vivienne,

The Hyde

who was very grateful for George's military efficiency, continuing on the secretarial side. Maureen from New Zealand came to stay for a few months to share in our life and to help in the ministry. She was a further help and her stay was eventually extended to eighteen months before she returned home to her homeland.

Despite this assistance, it was clear that Colin needed a holiday. Although in many ways the last thing he wanted was to go abroad by plane and stay in a hotel yet again, he also wanted to give the children an opportunity to do this. From the nearest travel agent he acquired brochures with details of some of the less luxurious package deals, and set about planning this surprise in secret.

"Mum, you didn't tell me Dad was going to Spain," said a puzzled Claire one evening. "Usually he always talks about where he's going."

I couldn't bear to actually tell her and spoil his surprise.

"You'd better ask him about it some time," I suggested, hoping she would forget about it.

She must have somehow worked out that there was more to this than met the eye, because on hearing him come in, she ran downstairs, and before he had got his coat off, blurted out, "Dad, why are there holiday brochures for Spain on your desk? I needed an eraser for my homework," she explained, seeing Colin dart a glance at me and wondering whether she should be feeling guilty for snooping around.

HIS GOD, MY GOD

From across the room I signaled that I couldn't help him very much.

"Claire was thinking you might be planning a tour over there," I said lamely, to give him time to think.

Colin ran his fingers through his hair. He looked so tired.

"I wanted it to be a surprise, darling. I thought we could all go together. Would you like that?"

"Oh, yes! Helen in my class went to Spain last year, and she said it was beautiful. But we can't afford it, can we?"

"No, not at the moment," admitted Colin ruefully. "But at least now you can help us pray about it."

So later that evening, with supper washed up, the whole family (but especially Claire) offered heartfelt prayers for our Spanish holiday. Having spent their whole lives surrounded by people who believed that God answered prayer, the children were less hampered by doubt. By the time they had finished telling the Lord all about it, the issue seemed to be wrapped up. I wouldn't have been surprised to find Claire deciding which clothes to take!

"I do hope they're not going to be disappointed," I whispered to Colin as we went to bed. "Once they get an idea in their heads . . . ."

I need not have worried. Once again, the next post included several large checks for which there was no specific need.

"There's even enough for me to have a new bathing costume," chortled the delighted Claire.

The Hyde

"What sort of plane are we flying in, Dad?" asked Clive, rushing off to look at the brochure again.

"Do they have ice cream in Spain like the seaside here?"

"Yes, Andrea." I smoothed back her fringe. "Lots and lots." Over their excited heads, Colin and I smiled with relief and joy at each other.

"No letters to dictate," he grinned.

"And no washing up."

Claire's faith was much strengthened by this answer to prayer and her earthly father was reminded that however lovingly he planned to give pleasure to his children, he couldn't outgive the Lord. That holiday was special to us, not because the brochure said so, but because it was a token of God's love.

If there was one message we needed to hear over and over again from the Lord, it was, *"Think big. Trust Me for more."* In many ways and from all quarters the whole household together was being challenged in this way. As usual, Colin led the advance.

During the summer of 1977, he had been asking the Lord to show him the way ahead, to give him more faith to fulfill God's purposes. In September he went to Australia, and while ministering in great power to huge gatherings of people, he was himself being renewed in faith. He was never happy to be static: God was always leading him into new adventures in faith, and was proving how faithful He is to those who put their trust in Him.

HIS GOD, MY GOD

He brought back with him a book called *A Daily Guide to Miracles* by Oral Roberts. Over the next few months we studied it as a household, working through practical assignments together. The principles of giving and receiving, and how God can bless both, were at the heart of this adventure.

We had always faithfully given away a certain proportion of our income, and in fact over the years this proportion had increased. Now we needed to learn that the more we gave, in time, money, talents and ability, the more the Lord could increase our vision of the ministry and the working of His power through it.

Here was the message again in another form: *"Enlarge the ministry."* Before long, we were applying this in very practical ways. There was so much work to be done, that we needed more help, both for Colin as he traveled around, and for the team left behind to look after the administration.

Colin had been working in our bedroom, and Viv typing away in the bedroom she shared with Maureen: a situation that couldn't go on for much longer. And it was obvious that the whole ministry needed to expand. God was giving Colin vision for that.

He came in for lunch one day holding a letter.

"Who's that from?" I asked, knowing he was going to tell me anyway.

"David Brown." David and Jane were the couple in Luton who had been filled with the Spirit as a "wedding present." David had become treasurer at St. Hugh's

The Hyde

and had a large part to play in the spiritual leadership of the church, as well as running an extended household. "The letter came on Saturday apparently," Colin continued. "Did Viv tell you about it?"

"No, she didn't." I squatted down to see whether the macaroni and cheese was getting brown enough under the grill. "Perhaps she didn't think it was very important. Is it?"

"Well, I am invited to go back to Luton to preach one Sunday. But that's not all," he went on, "because he says, let me see . . . ." Colin unfolded the letter and put it down on the table. " 'I hope at some point during the day to be able to talk to you about a concern which has been on my mind a lot recently.' " He looked up. "Does that make you think of anything?"

I paused in the straining of my peas to consider.

"Didn't you say some weeks ago that you felt the Lord was telling you to invite David to join you in the ministry?"

"Correct. And it's more than just the once a few weeks ago. I can't get the idea out of my mind. It's odd really, because he's had no theological training . . . ."

"Except under the Lord," I countered. "His experience in the church and his openness to the Lord are what really matters!"

"Precisely. I shall accept his invitation to preach, but he's going to get more than he bargained for!"

How we rejoiced when we learned that David and Jane wanted to discuss exactly the same idea! Unknown to each other, they had both been prepared

HIS GOD, MY GOD

for this step separately. Neither had mentioned it to the other because it seemed so far-fetched. It would be a big step for them to join us and forgo David's salary, but they did not waver. Their daughter Joanna was going to become a sister in June, and now they would be moving house about that time. Our first thought was that they should buy somewhere near us, and we should be praying for the money to rent offices nearby, but as soon as we looked at house prices in East Molesey, we abandoned this idea.

We began to pray for a house large enough for our two households which would be a suitable base for our expanding ministry.

A friend had a vision of Colin standing at the door of his family home near Bury St. Edmunds, which seemed to merit further investigation. The house was about to be sold. Our friend wanted to give us first option, but the rest of the family decided to put it up for auction. We would have to bid along with everyone else. The house was enormous, far beyond our anticipated needs, with so many bedrooms I lost count. I had all sorts of questions about its size, location and suitability. It would be suitable as a conference center but we were not being called to run such a center. Colin was to continue his itinerant work and the house was to enable that ministry. To my puzzlings over this, the only answer from the Lord was, *"Don't worry, just follow My plan as it is revealed to you. Step by step."*

Colin was to be in Canada when the auction took

The Hyde

place. Several urgent phone calls zinged back and forth between David and our household and it seemed that the Lord was wanting us to go to the auction. We had to leave very early to be on time. It turned out to be a scorchingly hot day as we sped aross the flatness of Suffolk.

"Well, this is an expedition of faith, if anything is," commented David wryly. "No sooner do I commit myself to trusting the Lord for everything than He sends me to the corners of the country to bid at an auction for a house with not a penny to spend." David was certainly being thrown in at the deep end. Not that we had any answers either.

The opening bid was extremely low, and eventually the lovely house was sold for a song, but not to us. We sat through the proceedings smiling, at peace. We were sure the Lord wanted us to be there, to see the house sold, and perhaps to witness to the owners, who expected us to be distraught and were much struck by our calm. We knew the Lord had brought us through a great test of faith and obedience. We returned home, our minds filled with the challenge from the Lord, *"Are you prepared to go wherever I lead you—even if it is to be a much bigger house than you think you need?"* Among other passages from the Bible, Isaiah 54 was constantly brought before us.

> Enlarge the place of your tent,
> And let the curtains of your habitations be
>   stretched out;

HIS GOD, MY GOD

> Hold not back, lengthen your cords and
>   strengthen your stakes
> For you will spread abroad to the right and
>   to the left . . . .

Our vision was being extended.

The next possibility was an even larger house in Lincolnshire, again ideal for conferences, with a private chapel in the garden. It was in need of a lot of restoration and would have been made available to us without having to buy it. But this wasn't the right place either. The Lord was showing us that our vision of what He would do in the years ahead needed to be bigger, but we still had to hold on to our purpose. The right house would serve our needs. We were not to create a ministry to serve the needs of the house. It was agreed that we should leave East Molesey by the end of August. Michael and June Barling, who were joining the Fountain Trust, were trying to buy somewhere to live, but were being guided towards taking over our house as we moved out. We were only there while the Trust, who owned the house, were no longer in need of it, and we had always known that. For the sake of our children and theirs, we wanted to move before the new school year started. But where to?

Towards the end of June, our sense of expectation rose to a new pitch: we were very tempted to provide for ourselves, but as we prayed we realized the danger of missing what the Lord was wanting to do. We fasted

The Hyde

and prayed for three weeks, eating only a light evening meal.

As we prayed He made it plain that we weren't to worry even about things like furniture—He would provide it all!

One of the conflicts I had to sort out before the Lord was my reluctance to move back into the hurly-burly of a larger household. I had much enjoyed the tighter family circle at East Molesey, and although the thought of increased fellowship was attractive, I still had to count the cost of this new move. It was obvious we were going to grow, and I would have to learn again how to balance my time so that I could support emotionally both my own family and any extensions to it. Previously, in Luton, this had involved me in a constant clash of priorities. Just because someone had a long tale of woe to tell, this didn't mean I could ignore all three children and their needs for an indeterminate period. Very aware of the risk of solving others' problems and creating larger ones in my children, I had to be constantly watchful. *"Will you trust Me even in this?"*

"Yes, Lord," I sighed, "even in this."

Others were also learning to hand over to the Lord their own particular fears, wrong ambitions and pockets of hidden doubt. As we shared what this time of purging and polishing was doing for each of us, the excitement grew.

In mid-July, Colin was partly responsible for the organization of a conference for charismatic leaders

HIS GOD, MY GOD

preceding the Lambeth Conference. He had little time to devote to the problems of housing, but he prayed with a group of leaders from all over the world, and they were given two pictures. One was of a hawk, apparently motionless, who suddenly dives, right on target. We were not to move until the time was right. The other was of a boat, tied by a piece of rope which had been frayed until only a very thin strand held it to the quay. It wouldn't be long now!

Colin phoned to pass on this news. I too had a picture to share with him.

"It's a house with an archway over the door, and a great climbing plant hanging down. I feel absolutely at peace."

"Isn't it remarkable? I do too. What's more, I think something is going to happen quite soon now."

At the weekend, the conference was opened to lay people as well. Colin was introduced to a lovely couple who had heard of our need and had a large house in Susex that they wanted to use for the Lord's work. As they talked, there was little doubt in Colin's mind that this was it. For a year they had been praying about how it was to be used, and the Lord had just told them to wait until His purposes for the house would be revealed. We arranged to meet at the house.

My heart was beating fast as we turned into the drive. I almost held my breath, then changed my mind about the wisdom of that as the drive went on and on, through trees with mossy banks on either side, round several turns, down a dip, then down a bit more and

The Hyde

over a bridge with a lake stretching away. I couldn't believe my eyes. Finally, we drove through a wrought-iron gate and pulled up in front of The Hyde. There was the door, with the ancient creeper over it just as the Lord had shown me.

Michael Warren and his sister Mary ushered us inside. The whole situation was like being in a dream. Wood paneling, heavily sculpted doors and a drawing room of generous and gracious proportions were all I took in. As we talked, everything fitted into place. It was as if all the decisions had been made by a higher authority. As the Lord had promised, the house was furnished, and we could move in as soon as we wanted.

We arranged to take the children and household there for a picnic, and I found I could convey nothing of the beauty of the place to them before we went. They would have to see it for themselves. I was grateful for the opportunity to see it again to prove it was real.

We were quite a large party. There were five Urquharts, David and Jane with Joanna and a newborn Jeremy, Viv, George and Hazel Hoerder, and three other friends who were staying with us. Once there we met the owners and their youngest child and a girl called Ginny who was staying with them. It could have been an awkward time, because the circumstances were so unusual, but we were made to feel very much at home. At first the children were subdued, but soon relaxed as we were left alone to show them the house. David and Jane wandered from room to room, dazed as I had been on our previous

HIS GOD, MY GOD

visit. We decided which rooms would be used for what, and where we would sleep, not quite believing that it would ever happen.

Outside again, it was a perfect summer day. We crossed the well-kept lawns to the formal lily pond, paved around the edges and surrounded by beds of roses. The scent of the roses and lavender added to the unearthly quality of the occasion. There we unpacked the picnic we had brought with us and were able to get to know the Warrens a little better. I was overwhelmed by their generosity. Together we marveled at the Lord's guidance, His timing, and His patience as He had taught us all to wait.

The next time I saw the house was the day we moved in. We could appreciate its beauty but were filled with a deep sense of unworthiness at the Lord's generosity, and the awesome responsibility of caring for the house and contents. This was a familiar feeling to me. Could I live up to what would be expected of me in such a place as this? I could tell that Viv was asking herself a similar question. At least we could be over-awed together!

We were praying one morning and had confessed our negative feelings when the Lord gave us a word of encouragement. It was a picture of cygnets looking gray and ruffled. Then they changed into beautiful swans. *"Yes,"* the Lord seemed to be saying, *"you feel you are unworthy of this place, but I am making you into beautiful swans."*

The image, and the promise, stayed with me for a long time.

10

Revelation at Last

The first few weeks at The Hyde were a time of adjustment, learning to live in such a large house. It took me so long to get from the kitchen to the bedroom and back that I would always try to work out several things I could achieve in the same trip, often remembering all but one errand I originally set out to perform. Then there was the problem of the stairs. At the front of the house, a wide imposing staircase rose gracefully to the first floor for the use of the gentry. At the back, leading from the servants' quarters to the kitchens, was a much more workmanlike set of stairs. This was fine if your social status was fixed. We all had to change constantly from hostess to housemaid. For weeks I had to pause each time I left our bedroom, trying to work out the fastest way down to a given point. Despite having to make this decision many times I day, I often felt, too late, that I had made the wrong choice!

The quantity of housework seemed overwhelming. Good team-work was essential, and we had new relationships to establish before this could work. The petty irritation of living with other people's methods had to be overcome, and for myself this meant coming to terms with the threatening fear that the other person could always do the job better than I could anyway. My low self-image took several blows as I compared myself with the apparently self-assured and confident people I was sharing the house with. We had been committed to the other members of the second household at Luton, and even more so at East Molesey, but now there was a sense of building a foundation that had to last, which gave us the awesome responsibility of perfecting our relationships. While we were still putting on some airs and graces, we could kid ourselves that it would be easy. It didn't take long, however, for our less sociable human natures to appear beneath the varnish, and it was easy to be negative in our thoughts both about ourselves and each other.

Every morning at 9:30 we met for prayer and praise: a very informal meeting since there weren't many of us. This was the natural point in the day to pick up and share with each other those lessons the Lord was teaching us. Colin had spent some time thinking about the effects of the negative emotions he knew most of us were feeling, and so began one morning a theme of his teaching which was to occupy us for some time.

"Could you find Ephesians, chapter one," he began. David, who always seemed so keen to learn spiritual truths that he gave the impression of sitting on the

Revelation at Last

edge of his chair, was the first to find the page. Seeing this, Colin asked him to read verse 3.

" 'Blessed be the God and Father of our Lord Jesus Christ, who has blessed us in Christ with every spiritual blessing in the heavenly places.' " David read slowly and thoughtfully.

"Thank you, David." Colin took a deep breath, then plunged in. "Nothing hinders faith more than the failure to appreciate who you are now that God has made you His child. Not that we have any rights of our own, as we all know well. We are sons of God only because of what He has done for us in Christ. His Father has become our Father; His inheritance has become our inheritance.

"By God's grace He has forgiven us and accepted us in His love." More than that, He has given us in Christ every blessing in heaven. He intends to appropriate those blessings, He wants to see them effective in our experience.

"Now, all these blessings that heaven has, are available only in Christ. That is where we are: that is where God has put us so that we can enjoy the full inheritance of our adoption as a son of God.

"And notice that the Scripture teaches clearly that God our Father *has* blessed us in Christ with *every* spiritual blessing in heaven. It is not a promise of what God says He will do, but a bold statement of what He has done, of what He has already accomplished. Whatever God has to give is yours already in Christ. Our faith can reach into the heavenlies and enable us

HIS GOD, MY GOD

to appropriate more and more of that inheritance while here on earth.

"Now, I realize that our experience doesn't always match up to this," chuckled Colin. I had wondered whether I was the only one to be thinking that this would be lovely in theory, but what about the practice?

"We know that our minds are often full of unholy, critical and unloving thoughts," Colin continued. "We do not see ourselves as we are in Christ, neither do we see others as they are in Christ. Let's turn to Colossians chapter three." A pause filled with rustles and someone clearing their throat. "Viv, would you read us the first two verses, please."

Viv's voice sounded light and high after Colin's. "Since, then, you have been raised with Christ, set your hearts on things above, where Christ is seated at the right hand of God. Set your mind on things above, not on earthly things."

"Right," Colin took up the baton again. "You see, Paul tells us here that we need to consciously set our minds on things above, on what the Spirit desires, on what is already ours in Christ. When our minds are filled with negative thoughts, we are not to dwell upon those thoughts, or to feel condemned for having them. We are simply to turn away from them immediately and fix our thoughts on things above.

"May I suggest that over the next few days, you search through your Bibles for anything it says about what we are in Christ. Then compare what you learn with the thoughts you have, and try to set your mind

Revelation at Last

on the word of God instead of on your feelings."

Colin closed his Bible and looked around at us all. "We'll continue tomorrow, but I think it's best to leave it there for now. Let's pray."

Colin's idea was taken up by everyone with varying degrees of enthusiasm, and towards the end of the week we discussed our finds. It was evident that our status and condition in Christ were a major theme of Scripture. But were we living in accordance with these truths?

Over the next few weeks we tried to reorientate our thinking and conversation so they became consistent with the Word of God. We agreed to help one another with this, not by flinging Bible texts at each other all the time, but by encouraging each other to see ourselves as God sees us. Along with everyone else, I found this extremely difficult to take at first. When I shrank from certain jobs I knew others could do better, like the big flower arrangements in the entrance hall, it was bad enough to remind myself that "I can do all things in Christ who strengthens me": but to have someone else point out the same idea was intolerable. I was afraid of failing, and would rather not even try, but the protective barrier of my own inadequacy, which shielded me from those jobs I feared, was being broken down. There was no good reason to avoid that tricky phone call any more. Everything had to be tackled.

"What I can't cope with," I confided to Viv one day, "is the nagging suspicion that I'm kidding myself. Surely if I'm afraid to do something, I'm silly to say

HIS GOD, MY GOD

that I can't be afraid because 'God has not given us a spirit of fear, but of power, love and a sound mind'? It sounds like the power of positive thinking."

"But which is truer," she answered carefully, "your emotions or God's Word? What you're doing is saying you know better than God. I know how you feel, but in the end what you're saying amounts to challenging the Word of God."

"Jesus is the Word, as well," I pondered, "so if we're not living in the Word, we're not living as fully in Christ as He wants us to."

"No, in fact we're living in accordance with the lies of the enemy."

In Romans 8 I found, "Those who live according to the sinful nature have their minds set on what that nature desires; but those who live in accordance with the Spirit have their minds set on what the Spirit desires. The mind of sinful man is death, but the mind controlled by the Spirit is life and peace." Then there was the glowing affirmation of Galatians 2:20. "I have been crucified with Christ and I no longer live, but Christ lives in me. The life I live in the body, I live by faith in the Son of God, who loved me and gave himself for me."

Each of us in The Hyde was being taught the lessons we most needed to learn. Indeed, many of the things we learned could not have been encountered in our normal family lives. Our commitment to Christ and to each other led us in new directions, probing our characters and challenging areas where we were slow

Revelation at Last

to admit the Lordship of Jesus. The development of the group became my development. Our experience was shared, we grew together and suffered any growing pains together.

In East Molesey I had always known what was going on. With a much larger group of people being involved, many responsibilities were handed over to others, and it seemed there were many more things I wasn't told. Organizationally it may have been of no importance, but emotionally I just couldn't cope with the idea. Time and time again I would hear about something long after everyone else, or so it seemed to me. "Why didn't anyone tell me that check had come in?" I would fume to myself. Although I usually said nothing, the issue soon became a sore point.

It was some time before it occurred to me that I should be praying about it, but finally I found the time to sit down and tell the Lord about it. "Why can't they understand how much it hurts?" I wondered. "Why does it hurt so much, anyway? Do I think I'm so important?" Gradually, as I prayed it through, my thoughts turned away from myself. The final question was, "What makes me think I have a right to know these things at all?" At last I saw that I needed to repent of my attitude which was basically proud and self-centered. As soon as I repented I found my attitude changed. I rejoiced when I was told something. And when I wasn't it didn't hurt anymore. I knew I would hear all I needed to, and I did.

This was just as well, because it was only one of

HIS GOD, MY GOD

many adjustments that we all had to make as time went by. "Change is here to stay" became a catch-phrase for those who had been there long enough to appreciate what was going on. Our roles seemed to be constantly changing.

It was to the advantage of everybody that we should have well-defined tasks, but for some people this involved some rather menial work. David, who had held a responsible job for many years, apparently became a beast of burden for Colin, trailing behind him with a briefcase or a box of books. In fact it was not quite as it seemed, because David was learning a great deal about the Lord and how to minister in the power of the Holy Spirit. Slowly he was being given responsibilities as he grew spiritually and felt able to take them on. Certainly he was never undervalued by those who knew him, and Colin grew to depend more and more on his support. To all outward appearances, however, serving the body of Christ was not a particularly glorious thing for David.

Viv not only did the secretarial work; she also cleaned the bathrooms. After Christmas we were joined by Ginny, who had been staying with the owners of The Hyde when we met them for the picnic. She had trained as an opera singer. Her initiation to community life took place in the kitchen garden, digging in manure and planting vegetables. Submission to each other and to the will of Christ took on a very practical form. For those who came in from the outside, there was always a testing time like this, when

Revelation at Last

independence had to be rooted out and interdependence grafted in.

Not that there were many new people for the first year. During that time we often prayed for a gardener, an odd job man, another secretary: there was so much to do. Slowly it became clear to us that for the moment we were complete. This was a foundational time, a time of building together, of learning slowly lessons we could help others with later. "Don't worry about all the jobs," the Lord seemed to be saying, "I'll send you the right people when you're ready. And I'll send individuals of My choice, not job-fillers. If you believed Me for the provision of this house, trust Me for this greater gift of the right people."

So it was that in the autumn of 1979 we were sent Charles and Joyce Sibthorpe with their five children, Frances and Marigold Pym with their four children, Kevin and Julie Stares and Cathy Franklin. Not that all these lived in the main house! By this time several estate cottages were available for us, so we were divided into households, but still came together daily for prayer, praise and teaching.

This marked the end of what we saw as our foundation year. With more help we could run The Hyde more efficiently for the visitors who often asked to stay, provide Colin with a better back-up team for his traveling ministry which was intensifying all the time, answer more letters from enquirers in depth and increase our involvement with the local area. So began a new era.

HIS GOD, MY GOD

We had been aware from the beginning of our time at The Hyde that we were responsible for making contact with the community around us, and particularly the village and parish of Handcross. As we got to know people, we invited the local vicar and a few others for a prayer and praise meeting. This evolved into a regular Tuesday night meeting, initially for the immediate vicinity. At first numbers were low, and the night only two came, it seemed silly to proceed. With time, this group grew, and a regular time of teaching was introduced. Because Colin was away so much, it was David who masterminded the operation, and Colin's presence or absence made no difference to the arrangement.

With the expansion of the community, others were now around to minister to the growing group. When the numbers reached about fifty, and the library was crowded beyond capacity, a dilemma was reached. The only place they could move to was the drawing room, but there they would have rattled in the vast spaces, and lost any sense of intimacy. The Christmas break was coming up. On the last meeting before Christmas, David announced that the first four meetings of the new year would take the form of a "Know Jesus" group, with Colin as speaker, and challenged each of the people there to bring an interested and preferably non-Christian friend with them. This was a double act of faith, because if all the people we were praying for arrived, we didn't have enough chairs for more than half.

Revelation at Last

Although there was no money available for the chairs, we ordered them and prayed, convinced that this was what the Lord wanted. On the Tuesday of the meeting, Francis was to set off for Cambridge to collect the chairs. At the prayer meeting that morning there was a jubilant shout of praise when Viv announced that the necessary sum had just arrived. What an encouragement to renew our prayers for the people to sit in them!

As we set out the precious chairs in preparation, the atmosphere in the drawing room was one of expectation. Would the very cold weather keep people from coming? The first people arrived, then more. There seemed to be plenty of people milling around, but looking round the door into the great drawing room, I saw they were scattered around the room with huge gaps between. More and more came however, and I was already praising the Lord when Viv whispered into my ear.

"I've just counted ninety people. Praise the Lord." Another check after the meeting had begun showed that the hundred we had prayed for had come. The next week and the week after one hundred and fifty came, and in the last week it leapt to one hundred and eighty. For the next two years we were to go on seeing the drawing room filled and overflowing out into the hall and even into the dining room opposite on most of the Tuesday evenings. We shared in some precious times of praise with this group, and were able to minister to both their spiritual and physical needs for healing as we grew in fellowship together.

With the sudden expansion of the community, we felt the need to go over the teaching we had done on being "in Christ." Although the last time around I felt I had heard it all before, this time I was much more open. The fact that I had begun to put it into practice meant that I was more receptive. I had believed that I was a new creation, and had struggled to make this real to myself in face of the truths I saw. Even though I saw myself as incapable, awkward, unreasonable, even unlovable, the continued bringing to mind of the Word of God began to have an effect. I realized I had stopped apologizing for the meal I had cooked. I began to accept that people might want to meet me as myself, not just as Colin's wife. It was a long time since I had hovered outside my own living room door in Luton, afraid to take coffee into the "Know Jesus" group.

Yet at this stage it was a question of naked faith and obedience. I believed the Word of God and rebuked my own emotions, which sometimes seemed to be jolly hard work. Were others having such a struggle?

As we worked through this teaching again two aspects of it came home to me in a fuller way. One was that we need to have our minds renewed. This process of constantly rebuking negative and unholy thoughts should become so automatic that eventually the Word of God is more real to you than any lies of the enemy. Paul says, "Do not conform any longer to the pattern of this world, but be transformed by the renewing of your minds." Secondly I understood in more depth that the source of my own low estimation of myself was coming from Satan, "the accuser of the brethren." In Christ I had absolute power over him when I confessed the Word of God and dismissed him.

At last the faith and obedience of the last months were crowned by a joyful certainty. I *was* in Christ! It *did* work! I *was* a new creation.

Now there came a new release of the Spirit in my life, and with it a new power—power over all those negative feelings. This is what it meant to live in victory!

Why ever had I, through unbelief, condemned myself to struggle for so long?

11

Hallelujah!

On many occasions after this turning point I was thrilled to realize how much the Lord had changed me since the chaotic beginnings in Luton. I looked back sometimes at the little molehills which had caused me so many problems. Where was the Caroline who never drove any distance without giving herself a headache from the tension of finding the way? Where was the vicar's wife who was intimidated to the point of trembling by meeting other clergy wives? What had happened to the housewife who could never be on top of things, and who carried a tremendous burden of guilt and inferiority? All these images of my past, and many others, were dead and buried. I was free to go forward.

Even as I praised the Lord for this, I knew that He wouldn't allow me to become self-satisfied. I might have climbed to a new place, from where the view was good, but sooner or later I would have to continue up the mountain.

Soon after this, the job of "hostess" for the visitors

was given to me. Colin's traveling ministry and the publication of his books had brought many people flooding to us for healing and renewal. There were always far more requests than we could deal with, but we met as many needs as we could. Each person would have periods of ministry as they needed, and I would see that they were being looked after for the rest of the time. In many ways I had been involved in this very practical ministry since the beginning, because we would all have been praying for each visitor and would be open to them as and when they wanted. Really taking this on as an official function was not a big step, but it was the thin end of the wedge.

This was a period of great expansion and continual change. As more families and single people joined the community in total commitment the structure had to change, and our places within the structure also.

David, who had long since been ready to run his own household, moved with Jane and Ginny into the village of Handcross, thereby allowing more room for visitors. We had shared a great deal together in praying in faith for The Hyde and then coming to terms with living there, and had grown to love one another. I would miss them first of all as friends. But I would also miss being able to share with Jane the responsibility of running the domestic side of things. It was all up to me now.

As new people came to join our household, I had to face each time the task of not only getting to know someone and live with them, but trusting them with my true self and loving them for what they were. For me,

Hallelujah!

perhaps because I was afraid of failing to love them the way Jesus would want, it was sometimes very difficult. In myself I knew I couldn't do it, and I learned that the love and unity which bound us together was not of our doing, based on natural affections, but on the Lord Who had guided us to be together.

One need, which became apparent over the ensuing months as more households came into being, was for smaller groupings within the community where we could live out more meaningfully the sharing of ourselves, our lives and resources. These groupings were called "cells"; each consisted of one large household or a number of smaller ones. There was a leader for each cell but because Colin was away so much, I not only took over our cell in his absence, but attended all the cell group leaders' meetings.

I slid into this so gradually that I didn't appreciate for some time what a miracle it was that it could ever have happened. Firstly it gave me, of all people, pastoral responsibility over those in the cell. There had always been someone to fall back on before, but now I had to learn to trust the Lord for myself. I was amazed that my timid and dithering former self could have been entrusted with the task. Secondly there was my voice.

If I was not tone deaf I was the next best thing to it. Whenever I launched into song the result was totally unpredictable, something often pointed out to me. To a certain extent I would play up to this, singing glorious pieces of opera horribly out of tune, but the fact was that I couldn't always find the right note. My inability to sing was partly physical, in my vocal chords, and partly emotional, fostered by years of failure and taunts, some light-hearted, others not so. When prayer and praise meetings became part of my life, practice improved things a bit. Now that we were meeting in our small groups I sometimes had to launch out and lead a chorus instead of simply following. And I could do it. It often amazes me still, but a real healing of memory, of inferiority and probably straight inability has taken place. Jesus is Lord of my vocal chords as well!

I saw this development as an outward sign of many more changes that were happening inside me. All the time I was being tested, taught that in myself I couldn't pass the test, and then given new strengths from the Lord. Each of us has continued to grow in Christ together.

An aspect of our common life about which we all had to learn, was what John calls, in 1 John, chapter 1, "walking in the light." We discovered that any problems in relationships could not be covered up for long. We were living so closely, not only in homes, but in our work, that any tension or bad feeling would be magnified. Before long it would be affecting us all, harming our corporate relationships to God and hindering what He wanted to achieve through us. We could not gloss over wrong attitudes. We needed to ask not only the Lord for forgiveness but one another. God wanted us to be transparent and open people living in truth and honesty, not just for our own sake,

Hallelujah!

but for His. He also wanted us to share with one another the problems we were facing in our spiritual growth so that we had no need to fear one another, but could support and pray for each other until we saw the Lord freeing us.

It was one of the recognized functions of the cell group that the unresolved situations be brought out into the open, so that we could pray together for the person concerned.

One morning, as I was preparing for the cell group meeting later in the day, there was one girl I couldn't get out of my mind. For months she had been sweet-tempered and loving, but recently a more unapproachable, snappy character had been coming through. I knew that I wasn't the only one who had recoiled, hurt, from what should have been a harmless conversation. "Wow, whatever did I do to deserve that?" I would muse to myself when she had swept out. I felt things were coming to a head, but didn't know what I could do about it. As I prayed the Lord gave me no clue. I just felt that we should begin by praising Him and hand the rest over to His more sensitive, capable leadership.

For a good half hour that evening the singing and prayer centered our thoughts firmly on the Lord in praise. Then, out of the silence that followed, a sentence was read from Hebrews chapter 12 by one of the men. He had no idea why, he confided later. He simply read it and waited.

"My son, do not make light of the Lord's discipline,

HIS GOD, MY GOD

and do not lose heart when He rebukes you, because the Lord disciplines those whom He loves, and He punishes everyone He accepts as a son."

That verse, electrified by the Holy Spirit, went home like a dart of light to the heart of this particular girl. Soon she was crying, and the person next to her put an arm around her shoulder while we all prayed quietly.

"Oh, Lord," she choked, and then cleared her throat. "Oh, Lord, please forgive me. For weeks I've been resenting the different jobs I've been asked to do. I've been angry with those who have asked me to do things. I thought I was too good to have to obey orders. I've been so proud. Please forgive me, Lord. Please forgive me, everybody."

She couldn't say any more, but she didn't have to. We all knew what it was to be broken like that. We all shared in the despair at ourselves and yet the joy there was in knowing we were loved, by God and by the others. And how I thanked the Lord for His timing, His prompting. He had no condemnation for her, neither did we. With much praise and hugging acceptance the matter was forgotten.

There were many meetings like this when the Lord worked in deep, emotional areas of our lives, but they were each forgotten quite quickly. We looked forward, not back. However little they became in memory, we all understood that small domestic details were just as much part of the Lord's concern for us as His daily provision of food and money, or His power and wisdom to conduct the great renewal meetings.

Hallelujah!

In fact, we found that we couldn't separate these areas from each other at all. Even as the community grew beyond our expectations, we were still living on the same faith principles which the Lord had guided us into in East Molesey, and which Colin had written about in *Anything You Ask*. And the Lord remained as faithful as we had discovered Him to be.

Sometimes, however, it seemed that money would be withheld as a means of showing us that something needed to be put right. On those occasions we would examine our hearts and confess any sin the Lord pointed out to us, seeking Him for direction. As we allowed Him to discipline us and set us firmly on our feet we would see the money coming in again. We had to recognize afresh that it came at the prompting of our Heavenly Father, and it lay within His power to leave us hungry if we stepped outside of His will.

This close link between the different aspects of the ministry was also a reassurance to me for another reason. My first role was and is that of being a wife to Colin and mother to Claire, Clive and Andrea. With all the hurly-burly and comings and goings of community life it was sometimes a conscious effort to keep this in view, but I knew that was my place. I wasn't involved in the traveling ministry with Colin and the others, although I, like everybody else, supported them in prayer. I still see myself as an ordinary person, but one for whom God has done great things. I am humbled and overwhelmed by what I have been caught up in.

HIS GOD, MY GOD

At the same time, so much of great spiritual importance was happening all around me that it would have been easy to see myself as a second-class member of the community, being based at home. Yet I knew, and the others knew, that each person, whatever their function within the community, was just as precious to God and could rely on Him for all they needed. I didn't need to struggle to be a spiritual giant. God wanted me where I was, and Colin wanted me as I was, and I could find fulfillment nowhere else.

Colin and the other three leaders felt exactly the same way about their positions. There wasn't any room for big-headedness or complacency. For a start, it was an overwhelming responsibility. They knew that they could never have engineered the developments that were taking place. In East Molesey as the Lord began to speak to us about enlarging, He had given the Scripture in Isaiah 54: "Enlarge the place of your tent, stretch your tent curtains wide, do not hold back; lengthen your cords, strengthen your stakes. For you will spread out to the right and to the left." From time to time this Word would come back and we would know that we needed to move into fresh areas, either physical or spiritual, in ways we didn't expect or necessarily desire.

Recognizing the great profit in teaching terms of writing books, Colin was anxious to commit his teaching about living in Christ to paper. By the time he sat down to it, he had taught it in depth twice to the community and numerous times to groups around the country. It had become such a key to his thought that it all seemed obvious now. The difficulty was to make it clear and fresh and, above all, practical. This made it especially hard to cloister himself away in the peace of his study and write. Outside those doors was a whole community of people to care for, to organize into a structure which allowed for growth, and what seemed to be a whole world clamoring for his teaching. Yet the best way to reach them all was through the book. From the past I knew that Colin would be totally absorbed in his work and often didn't get round to drinking the cups of tea I lovingly provided at intervals.

At last *In Christ Jesus* was finished. That did not mean the end of our problems, because its publication gave rise to a new wave of interest and more requests for personal teaching trips. Colin and his team, with David taking an ever more conspicuous role, toured up and down the country. When he returned, it was difficult for him to convey the glory and wonder of seeing lives made whole, bodies released from pain and personalities set free from the straitjacket of sin. Christians in many places were entering into their inheritance in Christ, and living in the power of that fact.

During 1980, Colin began to hear the Lord telling him that the great need for teaching could be met through cassettes, and that he should commit a systematic teaching course to tape. Many of the people who came to the various missions and meetings throughout the country and those who flocked to

HIS GOD, MY GOD

The Hyde were so hungry for ongoing teaching. Producing the course presented problems of finance and technology, but it was the Lord's idea, and with prayer both were provided. The first tapes were produced on a small copier and distributed that September to the hundred groups who had enrolled. We have never made any charge for the cassettes, or the worksheets which accompany them, and have looked to the Lord to make this possible. Our faith was really tested when, in time, we needed a much larger copier and a computer to handle the information about which stage every group had reached, but prayer once again released the necessary sums.

The appearance of the Kingdom Faith Teaching Course played an important part in the change that God was bringing about in Colin's traveling ministry. For years the team had been doing one-night stands, midweek meetings, sometimes a weekend. They centered their activities on the church which had invited them, and saw their aim as spreading the renewal. In an ideal world, a church would then have its own momentum and further growth through evangelism would result.

In fact, this was only happening to a limited extent, and Colin was given an increasing burden for the unsaved. The pattern of his ministry now changed. A whole area would be involved with the churches working together, and a week-long session of teaching and evangelism would be presented with a view to the non-Christian community. Each mission was prepared many months in advance, with leaders from the churches being invited to The Hyde to gain insight into what was needed, and to be bound in prayer and fellowship with the members of The Hyde team. In 1981 there were no fewer than twelve Kingdom Faith Missions in places as far apart as Blackpool and Tunbridge Wells, South Wales and Grimsby.

By 1982 there were 150 people attached to the community, living in many houses in the area. While my principal concern was for the members of my cell group, I also was able to help many others in their adjustment to community life.

Everyone whom we consider has been guided to join us arrives excited and full of great hopes. Some have doubts as well, and these are the realistic ones. However keen you are, however convinced that this is your niche in life, however lonely or frustrated you were before, committing yourself to community life is never a smooth process. Living in a parish, married or single, you can decide what to commit yourself to, and when life gets hard, or a relationship goes badly wrong, you can shut your door. Entering a common life means opening every possible door, and some you didn't even know existed. The loss of independence hits different people in various ways, but it hits most of us quite hard. Jolly fellowship is not the answer to everything unless you are prepared to work hard at walking in the light. This doesn't apply to relationships alone: being in bondage to a desire for marriage, for example, even if it doesn't affect your behavior, can block spiritual growth. The need to be thought of by others as important or indispensable might make you very useful for a time, but the final result is negative. All the past has got to go to the cross, be it your achievements, your salary or your stereo.

As people struggled with this adjustment, I learned to expect the Lord to help them, and show them the way. We would work at it in prayer together and encourage each other's faith. At that time it became obvious that a small leaders' group was needed to work under the elders, helping them in the day-to-day running of the fellowship. I was pleased, but surprised and fearful of the responsibility, when I was asked to share this with three of the men. This was another mark of recognition that I was continuing to grow in the Lord.

Since Andrea, our youngest, was now ten and there were many people the children knew well about the place, it seemed possible that I could leave them and accompany Colin on an overseas trip. We had both felt that with the constant change going on around them and Colin being absent so often that I should remain the constant factor in their lives. We were both very glad not to have to be separated, and for me to be able to share this important aspect of his life. In June 1980 I accompanied him on a two-week visit to the U.S.A. and Canada, and began to understand first-hand some of the problems I had been praying about during the previous tours. There were three conferences on this trip and I discovered what it was to move to several situations in quick succession and build relationships in a short space of time. We were hardly settled when we were whisked off to another place. Different personalities, different methods and above all the switch from a warm responsive congregation where we had seen the Lord's power and healing poured out upon His people as the conference progressed, to one which was completely cold. It was a great effort to start again from scratch.

While these experiences helped me understand Colin's tiredness when he returned, the Lord also put a few thoughts in my mind about the way we were living. More and more people were being raised up from the fellowship to minister to those who came to The Hyde, to the point where Colin's presence or absence made no difference to the ongoing work. It seemed the Lord was saying that we as a household no longer needed to live at the center of things. It certainly didn't make much sense for Colin to return from a long trip away to what sometimes seemed like Clapham Junction at its busiest.

Currents of dissatisfaction were running deep amongst the mission team early in 1981. The new format of mission to the unsaved was bearing some fruit, but many of the team involved yearned for more, and felt that the Lord wanted to do more. What could be wrong?

Many of us had read about revivals in Wales and other parts of the world, and felt strongly that a sense of the majesty and holiness of the Lord simply wasn't present as it had been during those times. What England needed was revival, but how could we take revival if we were not revived ourselves? We knew that despite our clear aim of walking in the light, more was needed.

It was decided that every member of the community should be asked to spend time during the Easter break asking the Holy Spirit to convict us of any wrong motive, intention or attitude of heart, and bring us into a new repentance. This was difficult; but each agreed that they should set time aside, even if they were away on holiday. On returning from that break many knew they were closer to God, but it was somehow incomplete. The Lord impressed upon Colin that we needed to meet with Him in His holiness. The first Saturday in May would be a day of prayer, and we would all meet together in the evening.

When we were together, we prayed, asking the Lord to meet with us. We spent some time in praise and worship, then fell quiet. Suddenly He was there.

Like reeds before a mighty wind, many of us could do nothing but flatten ourselves. Being on our knees was not enough. Majesty and holiness were there in their full naked power: it was devastating. Many wept as they recognized their sinfulness. Everyone felt dirty beside the purity of God, like white clothes stained with mud. Our one desire was to be washed, to get rid of anything that the Lord didn't want. We confessed our sin out loud, with no embarrassment. The Lord of Glory was present with such awe that everything else seemed irrelevant. Hours passed like minutes, and then it was over. We were just numb, amazed. We all hugged each other and went to bed, each of us trying to come to terms with what had happened.

The next night it happened again. And the next. Some people had missed the first two nights and the Lord obviously didn't want any of the fellowship to miss out. The Tuesday meeting for people from outside had hardly started when many became so aware of God's presence in His holiness that they wept before Him.

One visitor who missed that meeting arrived for the next with a puzzled frown.

"What's been happening here? I've always known The Hyde as a place of love and joy, but as I came down the drive I was aware of God's holiness as well."

As a community it changed us individually and together; we were free in a new way. Love flowed more freely among us as the attitudes of our hearts were changed. Now we were set on fire. Now we could take this revival to the needy world.

It also gave us a renewed vision for intercessory prayer. We had learned a certain amount about this before, but we knew now what it was to ask for the Lord's burden. Even sanctified imagination couldn't reveal the true nature of the battle that was to be fought, but the Lord could reveal that to us so that we could pray in greater confidence. More than that, we could pray until the victory had been won through prayer. In a human sense, the battle was about to begin

HIS GOD, MY GOD

when a mission started, but we could know that the outcome was decided in the spiritual realm. Those away on the mission would spend many hours in prayer, and we would support them as much as normal life at The Hyde permitted. No mission met with success that had not been prepared in this way, so we submitted ourselves to this discipline every time.

As for me, the revival was nothing like anything I had experienced before, and left me so conscious of any sin or wrong thought, that I couldn't get rid of it fast enough. Each fresh experience of the Lord is so loving, so personal, that you feel it is the ultimate. I had known breakthroughs before, but this was very different. Any words with which you describe spiritual experiences soon become over-used and meaningless. And then what are you going to call the next one? Yet a next one is what you desire.

For experience and obedience go hand in hand, and if we break the cycle at any point, we stagnate. I had learned to obey in many situations, but was I ready to move on again?

The vision for The Hyde as a center of ministry to leaders grew and grew. Michael and June Barling, who moved into the house at East Molesey when we left, were led to The Hyde to share in putting this into practice. It became increasingly clear that we were no longer needed to live in the house, and that the Lord was giving us a familiar message. *"Enlarge the ministry. Do not hold back."*

When we arrived at The Hyde three-and-a-half years

before, our minds were stretched to the utmost to believe that this was the house we needed. Our faith at that time could never have encompassed the idea of the growth that was to take place. We thought of The Hyde as a center for Colin's ministry. Now it seemed that it was needed for something quite separate which had grown from this. The space we were occupying there was valuable, and we had a different part to play. Our household was to find somewhere else. We spent many hours in prayer seeking confirmation from the Lord about this, but finally we were at peace and could go forward knowing it was right.

In February 1982 we moved into a house in a nearby village. This time the Lord provided not the furniture, but the money so that we could choose for ourselves! It was a gracious house, of generous proportions, with a peaceful atmosphere, and would provide the seclusion Colin sometimes needed as well as allowing easy access to The Hyde. It was large enough for our family plus four, including Viv, who had been with us through so many changes. There was also a flat above the garages which could be converted for further accommodation. We wouldn't be caught out by the need to expand this time!

Moving out of the big house was a real wrench. It meant a great deal to us, and embodied so much of what the Lord had been doing with us, that we felt as though we were leaving part of ourselves behind.

Yet as I looked back, had I not felt the same about Luton? Certainly knowing what I know now, I can see

HIS GOD, MY GOD

that to stay there would have been to block God's purposes for us, and deprive us of everything that has happened since.

Again, what is a house, after all? With the rumpus of the first community and the calmer period that followed, the Lord had taught us that our home was His, to use as He directed. Whether it was cigarette holes in the sofa, or fold-away beds in the study, the message was the same. Surely I hadn't forgotten that lesson.

Then I remembered the many occasions when the Lord had given us the relaxation and enjoyment that we needed for a balanced life: the boat, the Spanish holiday. I knew in my heart that a more secluded home was essential for Colin.

Above all, the Lord was moving on. Choosing not to follow is always a possibility, always a temptation. How many times have I wanted to hold on to what is familiar, secure? Would I refuse to face the next step? It was unthinkable.

As I write from the new house, six months later, it is becoming clear that new developments are under way again. The sound of splintering glass from across the lawn witnesses to the fact that the conversion work on the flat has begun by breaking down and clearing away. Once again the whole community is facing the fact that the Lord always needs to be allowed to clear out the old in our lives to make room for the new.

Above the door of our home, carved in the mellow stonework of the lintel, is a line from Psalm 127.

Hallelujah!

> Except the Lord build the house, they labour in vain that build it.

It was carved there many years ago, but God's truth is eternal. In whatever happens in the future, we must live out that principle. Without God, we are nothing. Yet if we make our lives available to God in obedience and love, He can do anything with them for the sake of His Kingdom.

The outworking of this obedience will be different for each of us, but for Colin and me, for you, the challenge is the same.